YOUR
FINANCIAL REVOLUTION

The Power of Generosity

GARY KEESEE

Published by Free Indeed Publishers.

Distributed by Faith Life Now.

Faith Life Now
P.O. 779
New Albany, OH 43054
1-(888)-391-LIFE

You can reach Faith Life Now Ministries on the Internet at www.faithlifenow.com.

DEDICATION

This book is dedicated to my beautiful wife of 40 years, Drenda. She is the most generous person I have ever met. She is always thinking of others and has taught me so much about loving people, for which I am forever thankful!

—Gary Keesee

TABLE OF CONTENTS

INTRODUCTION..09

CHAPTER 1: The Power of Generosity.......................................17

CHAPTER 2: The Answer: Grace..35

CHAPTER 3: Do You Qualify?...63

CHAPTER 4: Whose Money Is It?..79

CHAPTER 5: You Need a Partner!...95

CHAPTER 6: The Mystery of the Tithe....................................109

CHAPTER 7: You Need a Purse: Part One.................................129

CHAPTER 8: You Need a Purse: Part Two.................................161

CHAPTER 9: The Law of the Measure.......................................173

CHAPTER 10: The Generous King..189

CHAPTER 11: The Promise to Those Who Are Generous........201

INTRODUCTION

When God called Drenda and me to do TV, I will have to admit it was the furthest thing from my mind. I had just returned from Albania, where I conducted five sessions on the Kingdom of God and told them how Drenda and I became debt free following the laws of the Kingdom.

If you have read my previous books, you might remember how the blue haze of God's glory filled the missionary's living room the night we did the last session. It was there the Lord spoke to me, "*I am calling you to the nations to teach people my covenant of financial blessing. And wherever I send you, I will pay for it.*"

That night changed my life. However, I had no idea exactly what the Lord meant by His words, "*I am calling you to the nations.*"

As I was to find out, television would be the means the Lord had in mind. Again, that is not something I would have thought of doing or even desired to do. The one thing I did know for sure was that I was passionate about helping people discover what Drenda and I discovered—the Kingdom of God.

It had been nine years of living in severe debt, living with liens of all types, and fighting debilitating panic attacks. The antidepressants the doctors put me on did not help. I found myself withdrawing from life, and the darkness of fear seemed to invade every thought. I was so bound by fear I even got to the place where I was afraid to leave my house, which obviously did not do well for my sales business. We were quickly fading into bankruptcy, and I seemed powerless to stop it. Shame was now a way of life, and I felt like such a failure. The greatest failure I felt was to my beautiful wife and children. Besides not providing the money we needed, I was not a great father or husband during those years.

We survived by living in an old 1850s farmhouse where everything was broken. The windows were held together with duct tape. The carpeting on the floor was found along the road in a trash pile. The mattresses in my boys' room were found in a nursing home's discard pile. The cars we drove were a disgrace. Our lives were filled with constant collection calls from attorneys and the multitude of credit card companies and loan companies we owed money to.

I was hopeless! Yes, I was a Christian who loved God. I went to church and was baptized in the Holy Spirit. I had an Old Testament Bachelor's degree and one year of Bible school under my belt, yet something was wrong, terribly wrong!

In desperation one day, I cried out to God, and immediately He answered. It was not like I had not prayed during those nine tense years; I had. But this time, I *knew* I needed to hear.

I guess up until that time, I always thought I could pull myself out of the financial hole I had dug by doing things in my own strength. But that morning I knew I was done. I had borrowed from every friend I had, borrowed tens of thousands of dollars from family, and every means I had to gain more credit was ruined.

When I prayed that morning, I was desperate, and yet surprised that I heard his reply so quickly. Up out of my spirit I heard Him quote to me Philippians 4:19:

> *And my God will meet all your needs according to the riches of his glory in Christ Jesus.*

I said back to the Lord, "Lord, I know that verse, but I do not see that happening in my life." He spoke again and told me that the reason I was in this mess was because I had never learned how His Kingdom worked. I did not know what He meant by that, but Drenda and I were determined to find out.

One of the first Scriptures that God showed us was Luke 6:20:

> *Looking at his disciples, he said: "Blessed are you who are poor, for yours is the Kingdom of God."*

The Kingdom of God was our answer?! Again, we really had no clue what He meant by that, but we knew we needed to find out.

We will talk more about the Kingdom in a minute, but let me tell you what the result was.

The Holy Spirit began to show us things in the Bible that we had never seen before. By applying what the Lord was teaching us about the Kingdom, we were able to get completely out of debt in two and a half years. We began to pay cash for our cars and bought 55 acres of land with cash, land full of beautiful hardwoods and marshes where I could hunt and raise my kids in the great outdoors.

And one of my greatest joys in life was watching Drenda design and build her dream home, which we own debt free as well.

After what I had been through and after we saw the Kingdom of God operate like it did in our lives, we lived in a state of celebration *every day*. In fact, the party has not stopped. We are still celebrating the Kingdom every day. Going from digging under the couch cushions to find a few dimes to buy a Happy Meal for our kids to now being debt free and able to give hundreds of thousands away to help spread the Gospel around the world is definitely cause for celebration.

Drenda and I are so passionate about telling people about God's amazing Kingdom. This was the reason I went to Albania in the first place.

As I mentioned, when God spoke to me in Albania about going to the nations, I was confused. What did that mean? At that time, I was pastoring the church that Drenda and I had started ten years earlier. Was I to resign from the church and start traveling?

Through a maze of God ordained introductions, Drenda and I were introduced to people who were doing television and to companies that did TV production work. It's not that I was looking for them; God just brought them along our path. Again, I had no interest in doing TV at all, but I remembered a vision I had several years earlier. I was praying at one of our church services when, suddenly, the Lord told me that I would be doing TV and radio. I did not think much of it since I really had no interest in either at the time, but it caught my attention, and I told Drenda about it.

To make a long story short, God opened some amazing doors and brought some amazing people along our path that encouraged us to do TV, yet we knew nothing about TV. *And when I say nothing, I mean nothing.* But we felt we needed to keep following what God was showing us.

We had no equipment and didn't even know what equipment was needed to do TV, but the people that God was bringing to us did. Eventually, we came to the place where we had to make a decision. A TV production company offered us a contract to do the production work at a discounted rate. Counting air time and all the costs involved to actually start TV, we figured it would take about $300,000. That was $300,000 we did not have at the time. But after praying about it and wrestling with God about it, I finally said yes. (Of course you never win a wrestling match with God).

So the production company came into town (they were based in Texas), and we started to film our first TV program. Since we did not have a set, we basically filmed our entire first year in our living room in front of the fireplace. To say I was nervous going into that first taping is an understatement. I did not know what to expect. And it was not just doing the actual TV taping that caused me to be anxious. I had to come up with all the content and basically put the whole program together, along with Drenda's input of course. The production team gave us some great advice and coached us, but I was still not comfortable.

Please understand that I am not naturally an outgoing person, so for me to do TV was totally out of my comfort zone. Besides that, the production team was extremely distraught the day of the taping. The head of the team had left in the middle of the night because his young son was killed after being hit by their neighbor's car in the driveway. They told me that morning just before we were to tape. I decided not to tell Drenda until after the taping. Wow, that was tough.

Then, directly after the taping, one of our staff was riding my son Tim's dirt bike and crashed it. Tim came running into the house yelling that David was dead. He was not dead, just knocked out, but what a way to start off.

We survived the week of taping, and the show went on the air on a local station. We continued taping one week a month, but by the end of the second month, it was not getting easier; and I was struggling with feelings of inadequacy and panic all at the same time. I finally told the production company owner I could not do this. He stared at me for a moment and said, "NO! You must do TV!"

He then told me to take a seat because he wanted to show me something. He turned the television on and turned to the Christian block of TV networks. To be honest, I had really never watched a lot of Christian TV, but what I saw that day made me sick and made me rethink even being involved with Christian TV at all.

On one program, they were selling "holy olive oil" that they claimed would bring a greater anointing to prosper. On another, the preacher was selling "anointed wafers," stating that you would get a new revelation with every bite. On another show, I heard that if you gave in the next three minutes, you would get a triple anointing to prosper. In another, freeze-dried food was offered. Every show seemed to offer some kind of weird incentive to get people to give.

But the missing part I noticed was that none of them told the people how to receive what they needed—how the Kingdom actually works. They were telling them they needed to sow a seed, but I knew that someone needed to tell the people how to *harvest* that seed!

There were many pieces of the puzzle that people needed to learn if they were to be successful. By simply just teaching people how to give and not how to harvest, I knew that people would become disillusioned with God and think He had failed them when things did not happen the way they expected them to.

People needed to know the laws of the Kingdom and why giving is such a vital part of walking in the Kingdom's abundance here in the earth realm. And again, more importantly, they needed to know what to do *after* they gave. They needed to know how to harvest what they needed from God.

I discovered that I have my part to play in my harvest—the first of which was to learn what faith was and why it was needed. I needed to learn how the Holy Spirit leads me to my harvest and how important timing and the details of my harvest are. I discovered that there are spiritual laws that needed to be learned and applied as well as laws governing the natural realm that would impact the harvest.

All of these programs made it sound like the money was just going to show up in your mailbox.

I will agree that sometimes it *does* show up in your mailbox, but if you examine those cases closely, you will find spiritual clues as to why and how it showed up.

After watching a few of these programs, I was embarrassed by what I saw. No wonder the world was not paying attention. But I was also angry. I realized at that moment that I was needed, that I had something to say.

I decided to continue on with TV because I had a story to tell. And I have continued to do TV now for the last 14 years and have seen tens of thousands of people discover the Kingdom—not religion but the Kingdom—and they have had the same kind of results that Drenda and I have had.

I know you will have the same results as well.

This book, *Your Financial Revolution: The Power of Generosity*, is the fifth and final book in my Financial Revolution Series. I am excited about the complete series, and I am excited about this final book.

As in all my previous books, you'll see I take some time in the beginning to bring people who may not have read the other four books up to speed with some review. NOTE: If you have read my other books, you can skip chapter 7a. Or if you want to review, which I suggest, then start at the beginning in chapter one.

—Gary Keesee

CHAPTER 1
THE POWER OF GENEROSITY

Our family was eating dinner one night at one of our favorite local restaurants. The waitress was a young lady who was very pregnant. As I was about to pay our bill, I suddenly felt led to give her a big tip instead of the 22-25% I usually give, so I added $100 to the tip amount. She picked up the signed Visa slip without looking at it and walked back toward the kitchen.

In a minute, she was back, with tears streaming down her face. She came back to thank us. She told us how she was in a tight financial situation and was wondering how she could make it. We had the opportunity to share Christ with her and pray for her before we left.

We did nothing but be generous to open the door of ministry to her heart.

> *Or do you show contempt for the riches of his kindness, forbearance and patience, not realizing that God's kindness is intended to lead you to* **repentance**?
> —Romans 2:4

The King James Version of Romans 2:4 says that God's goodness leads us to repentance.

Being generous is acting like God does.

Matthew 5:45 says:

> *That you may be children of your Father in heaven. He causes his sun to rise on the evil and the good, and sends rain on the righteous and the unrighteous.*

God is good, and He is generous! We are his children, and our new nature in Christ is one of being generous as well. As in the story above, being generous is sharing God's heart for people. Like taking a sip of cold water on a very hot day, being generous brings relief and hope to a world that is in the desert of poverty.

The impact of giving freely is clearly seen in Paul's instruction in 2 Corinthians 9:10-15, written to the church in Corinth:

> *Now he who supplies seed to the sower and bread for food will also supply and increase your store of seed and will enlarge the harvest of your righteousness. You will be enriched in every way so that you can be generous on every occasion, and through us your generosity will result in thanksgiving to God.*
>
> *This service that you perform is not only supplying the needs of the Lord's people but is also overflowing in many expressions of thanks to God. Because of the service by which you have proved yourselves, others will praise God for the obedience that accompanies your confession of the gospel of Christ, and for your generosity in sharing with them and with everyone else. <u>And in their prayers for you their hearts will go out to you, because of the surpassing grace God has given you. Thanks be to God for his indescribable gift</u>!*

Your generosity causes people to praise and thank God!!! Notice that Paul says that being generous is your *service* to God.

The definition of the word service is: *The performance of work or duties for a superior or as a servant.*[1]

It is part of your duty on God's behalf, here in the earth realm, to share His heart and concern for people. The result is clear—it touches people's hearts and opens them up to receive Christ.

I think we can all remember when someone came to our aid and how much it meant to us.

I can remember owing $4,000 in taxes when I was first married and had no idea where I would get the money. I lay awake many nights dreading the situation I was in. We lived in Tulsa at the time and had planned to visit Ohio for the holidays.

When my dad asked me how things were going, I told him about the IRS bill. He said, "Well, that is easy to fix," and he pulled out a check and wrote it to me for the entire amount. His instant generosity to me at that moment caused me to love my dad even more than I did. For in that moment, I saw his heart for me.

My dad often kept his heart hidden. He never really showed his emotions openly to people, not even to my mom. My dad had never told me he loved me my entire life up until that point, as far as I could remember. Only once when my mother told him to say it did he finally say it, and after much drama. I can remember that day like it was yesterday. Mom was pleading with him, saying, "You cannot tell your own son that you love him?" But he remained quiet.

Finally, with my mom in tears, he told me he loved me. But I never counted that one moment in time as him telling me he loved me because he was coerced to do so.

---

[1] *The American Heritage® Dictionary of the English Language, Fifth Edition*

Instead of telling us verbally that he loved us, there were times when my dad would buy us something special, and I think all four of us children knew that dad loved us. I would only see Dad's heart by what he did, almost never by what he said. I held those moments dear as they stood out like lights in a dark night to me.

The day he wrote the check for the IRS debt, my heart was filled with gratitude. In tears, I hugged my dad and thanked him. His response caught me off guard. He said, "As long as I have it, I want to help."

I am sure you have memories of someone's generosity like I do, moments that caught your attention. So, make this mental note:

Generosity shows people your heart and God's heart for them.

Generosity is so powerful. It supersedes words and goes straight to the heart. It's amazing how we can remember a compliment that someone gave us, or a gift.

One of the first moments in my life that I saw my dad's heart was when I was in sixth grade. My cousin and I were into model rockets at the time, and I had purchased one with a clear nose cone that you could put things into and launch them into the sky.

This one particular day, my cousin and I thought we would put a frog in the nose cone and tape the nose cone on so that the rocket would crash instead of opening its parachute. The intent was to see what would happen to the frog, which I think you can imagine.

Well, we launched the rocket and, to our horror, my dad had come outside to watch. We knew he would not be pleased with our murder of a frog.

The rocket went up just like it was supposed to and then arched over and came down nose first into the ground. As I went to pick it up, I saw that the nose cone was smashed and the frog was dead, as I expected.

As I picked up the rocket, I quickly tossed the dead frog aside to hide our true intentions from my father. He walked over and asked for the rocket. I can still remember his very real concern for our rocket. As he held it in his hands, he began to tell me how I could fix it and how sorry he was that it crashed. He then went into detail on how I could rebuild the broken pieces. The actual care in his voice and kindness convicted me of my wrongdoing. He never did know of the frog, but I never forgot his gentle concern for me and my rocket. It stood out to me at that moment that he really did care for me.

Then there are times that God uses people that we do not even know to encourage us and reach out to us.

A time that was especially memorable was the time that Drenda and I went pheasant hunting with some friends. Drenda and I had just gotten married and were living in Tulsa. One of my roommates lived in Kansas and invited us to join him on that year's annual opening day pheasant hunt. I was thrilled to say the least.

We drove the five hours to Kansas, had a great day of hunting, and got our limit of birds. But on the way back to Tulsa, our friend's car engine blew. We were in the middle of nowhere on a dirt road and still hours from home. If you have ever been to Kansas, then you know how barren it is.

It was now dark, and we only saw one light off in the distance. We hiked to the farmer's home and told him of our situation. I was totally shocked when he said, "Well, I will drive you home tonight. I will put your car on my trailer, and I will get you home in time for work on Monday." (Drenda was to start a new job in the morning working part time at a restaurant, and she was so disappointed that she might have to call in and say she was unable to be there.)

Amazingly, this man, who we had never met before, drove us five hours home to Tulsa and then turned around and drove all the way back to Kansas before morning. He drove all night!

I will never forget that selfless act of kindness. He would not even take a penny for the gas. I will always be grateful to that man. When I think of him, I always think of his gift with gratitude.

When people think of you, they are going to thank God for your generosity.

I am sure that you can think of situations like these in your own life. You will remember how grateful you were for the care and concern someone showed you. Well, this is what Paul was trying to convey to this church—their generosity was reaching people with the heart of God and causing people to give praise and thanksgiving to Him for their service to him.

PEOPLE ARE GOING TO THANK GOD FOR THE SURPASSING GRACE HE HAS GIVEN THOSE WHO ARE GENEROUS!

When I came to Christ, I found that my heart softened, and I saw that I truly cared for people. When I saw a need, I always wanted to help, but it was so frustrating that I usually couldn't because I had no money that I could spare.

I have found that this is really how most people feel as well. Just speak up in a crowd and ask for directions, and you will have a dozen people wanting to help you find your way.

But as I discovered in the Bible, being generous is more powerful than I ever realized. Reading this passage in 2 Corinthians 9 revealed a Kingdom law that changed everything I thought about giving:

> *This service that you perform is not only supplying the needs of the Lord's people but is also overflowing in many expressions of thanks to God.*

Because of the service by which you have proved yourselves, others will praise God for the obedience that accompanies your confession of the gospel of Christ, and for your generosity in sharing with them and with everyone else.

And in their prayers for you their hearts will go out to you, because of the <u>surpassing grace God has given you</u>. Thanks be to God for his indescribable gift!

—2 Corinthians 9:12-15

People are going to thank God for the surpassing grace He has given those who are generous!

To truly get a handle on what Paul is saying here, we need to define our terms.

Surpassing means: of a large amount or high degree; exceeding, excelling, or extraordinary: <u>*structures of surpassing magnificence.*</u>[2]

What is going to be yours in a huge amount? What is going to be extraordinary and surpass magnificence in your life? God's grace!!!!!

Okay, now we need a definition for grace.

Grace means God's unmerited favor.

This is the standard definition of grace, but it falls so short of what it really is. Let me give you a better definition.

The following is a quote from Wikipedia about divine grace:

Common Christian teaching is that grace is unmerited mercy (favor) that God gave to humanity by sending his son to die on a cross, thus delivering eternal salvation. However, this definition alone may not cover all uses of the term in scripture. For example, Luke 2:40 (King James Version), "And the child grew, and waxed strong in spirit, filled with wisdom: and the

---

[2] Dictionary.com

grace of God was upon him." In this example when using the definition of grace to mean unmerited favor it does not make sense that the sinless Christ would need this.

James Ryle has suggested "Grace is the empowering Presence of God enabling you to be who He created you to be, and to do what He has called you to do." Alternatively, Bill Gothard has suggested "Grace gives us the desire and the power that God gives us to do his will." Both of these definitions make good sense of the word grace throughout the Bible.[3]

So, we see that what Paul is talking about in this passage is the grace, or the empowerment, to prosper. This gift, the gift of grace, was celebrated because it empowered the people to prosper. And as they in turn were generous, meeting people's needs, it caused them to worship God.

Paul ends his discussion with, "**Thanks be to God for his indescribable gift!**"

Okay, one more definition. The word indescribable means, as it clearly indicates, that there are no words that can adequately describe it.[4] That is how good Paul said the gift of grace was, *beyond words*, and especially to those who were ministered to by the finances that it provided.

Here is the power that can set you free from financial bondage. This power, the grace of God, is available to every believer.

But here is the issue. We can spend a lot of time talking about what Paul said to do—to *give*. But if we do not understand grace, the empowerment to prosper by the power of God, we miss the harvest God intended for us. It would be like planting your garden in the

---

[3] https://en.wikipedia.org/wiki/Divine_grace

[4] *American Heritage Dictionary of the English Language, Fifth Edition*

woods under the shade of a big tree—there is no sunshine, no power to bring forth the desired result.

Drenda and I would read stories in the Bible where the power of God showed up and completely changed the situation for the good. I will have to admit that we heard very few such stories occurring in our church as we grew up. Outside of salvation, no one really ever talked about how to bring the grace of God into a situation.

Now, I understand that our salvation is the most important thing. But as I just mentioned, I needed that same grace to function in *every* area of my life, but I did not know how. And because of my ignorance, we were broke, sick, and depressed. We knew of salvation—we had the eternal salvation part down—but we did not know or understand how to bring heaven into our lives and to manifest the power of God. As I told you, we were a financial wreck!

But this is what the Lord was telling me that day when He spoke to me concerning the Kingdom, "*You are in this mess because you have never learned how My Kingdom operates!*"

In other words, He was saying that I did not know how to release the authority of the King here in the earth realm. I had never learned how or even that I could. I had no idea how to tap into the grace, the power of God.

Oh, by the way, there was more to that conversation that day when God spoke to me about the Kingdom. He went on to say, "*My church is living just as the children of Israel did when they were slaves, making bricks for Pharaoh. They are slaves! My people are in debt, and I want them free!*"

Let me make a point here: You will never be free until you are financially free. And as Drenda and I have said for the last 30 years, you will never discover who you really are and walk in the spiritual purpose for your life until you fix the money thing.

And let me make this point also: **YOU CAN GET FREE!**

I proved it, and thousands of others have as well. God's grace is there to help you. There are things you are called to do that you will never be able to accomplish as a slave. You must get financially free not only for yourself and your family but also so people can see the Kingdom of God operating in your life, and, like a fruit tree laden with ripe fruit, it will attract people to the Kingdom.

PEOPLE ARE LOOKING FOR ANSWERS. THEY ARE LOOKING FOR THE REAL DEAL. THEY DESPERATELY NEED TO SEE THE KINGDOM AND NOT RELIGION.

People are looking for answers. They are looking for the real deal. They desperately need to see the Kingdom and not religion.

Let me tell you about a conversation I had with a nurse the other day. Well, actually two nurses.

My mother is 88 years young and is doing quite well, but she needs help getting around, as you can imagine. So, this particular day, I was to take her to several doctor's appointments.

As I was talking to the nurse at the first appointment, she began to ask me what I did for a living. I told her about our church and also about my financial company and how we help people get out of debt. Well, that caught her attention. She went on to tell me that she was in trouble, maxed out in debt, and had no idea how she was going to survive.

When I went to the second doctor's appointment that day, I had nearly the exact same conversation with the nurse there. She actually had tears in her eyes as she was telling me about her financial situation.

Friend, they are not unique. This is how America is living today.

My heart and passion are to help people understand that there is a better way to live life—the Kingdom way.

When Drenda and I began to learn about the Kingdom of God and began to apply what God was teaching us about the Kingdom, our lives changed drastically. We began to see that grace Paul was talking about showing up in our lives.

One night, I had a dream to start our own business helping people get out of debt. That is crazy, right? I mean the poster child for what never to do with money is now running a company showing people how to get out of debt. Only God, right?

You may be asking, "How did that happen? How did you know how to get out of debt so that you actually would be able to help other people get out of debt?" That is a great question!

To make a long story short, the Holy Spirit showed me how it could be done.

Of course, I had things to learn in the natural world, and then I had to have people coach me on how to set up my company, but the Holy Spirit directed the progress and the unique strategies and methods we used to help people. That company took off and is what funded our financial freedom.

By the way, I know what you are thinking: We must have charged a lot of money for that help if it provided all the money we needed to be free.

Nope. As I said, the Holy Spirit gave us a very unique business model, and here it is:

We work with our clients for FREE.

How can I charge a fee to someone who is already struggling to pay their bills to help them get free? No, I just cannot do it. God gave me a different way of funding my company. There was and never will be a charge for my company to develop a customized plan for clients to be debt free. My company specializes in showing clients how to be debt free in less than seven years, including their home mortgage, usually without changing their income.

We are supported not by our clients but by dozens of companies, vendors, and professionals that we have picked to provide solutions and restructuring options for our clients. They support us for telling our clients about them.

For instance, in our restructuring process, if I know that company XYZ can cut my client's insurance bill in half, I am going to tell them to check out company XYZ. My client can now talk to XYZ for themselves and make up their own mind and make their own decision if they are interested in XYZ's cheaper rates as part of their restructuring plan or not.

So, for the client, everything is free. And I am sure this was a main contributing factor in the awesome growth of our company. Check out our company at forwardfinancialgroup.com.

We also help people discover what I call safe investing. It is what it sounds like: investing with no risk of market downturns stealing their precious retirement money.

I said all that to say that over the past 30 years, we have talked with hundreds of thousands of people, and we have seen the mess that most Americans are in.

One example sticks out to me and illustrates how a lot of Americans live.

A lady called me to visit her, as she needed help with her debt. I, and one of my associates, met with her, and I sat there in disbelief as she explained her situation. She had *32* different credit cards, all maxed out. (Yes, you heard that right—she had 32 credit cards.)

She had successfully built her own prison, and she was asking me for the key to get out. In my mind, the answer was easy: Stop using credit cards. That would be a good start. So, I told her to cut up the cards and insisted that she live within her income. Then I gave her an assignment to make a list of all her living expenses so I would know where to start in counseling her. I also suggested she start using a debit card instead of a bank card to avoid making her situation worse.

At the suggestion to cut up her cards, she instantly burst into tears and asked this shocking question: "How will I be able to buy shoes?"

Did I hear that right? She did not have enough money for food, but she was asking about shoes?

You may think that lady must be an anomaly. In the number of credit cards she had, she was. But in being in financial prison, she is not. Look at the latest stats in America:

- 57% of people do not have $1,000 in the bank.[5]

- 44% cannot pay an unexpected $400 bill.[6]

- 23% of Americans cannot pay their monthly bills and are falling further and further into debt every month.[7]

Friend, Americans are just as God told me—they are slaves.

Think of what a slave does.

---

[5] Ray Hanania, "57% of Americans have less than $1,000 in Savings, March 31, 2021, SuburbanChicagoland.com

[6] Joseph Lawler, "44 Percent of Americans Couldn't Cover an Unexpected $400 Expense," *Washington Examiner,* May 19, 2017.

[7] Megan Leonhardt, "Become Debt Free," May 24, 2019

- He does not work for himself. Although he (or she) is working and producing profit, the profit is sent to lenders each month, leaving just enough for the family to survive another month.

- Slaves live in houses they do not own (meaning they have a mortgage).

- They drive cars they do not own to go to work to pay for the house they do not own.

- They wear clothes they bought on the credit card to go to work, to pay for the car and the house they do not own, along with the student loan they are still paying off from 20 years ago.

You get the idea.

> *The rich rule over the poor, and the borrower is slave to the lender.*
>
> —Proverbs 22:7

Did you know that most people do not like their jobs? Actually, a Gallup poll says that 85% of employees hate their jobs.[8]

Why then do they work where they work? Because they are slaves, and slaves do not have options!

So, is there a way out of slavery? Yes!

Don't believe me? Let me show you.

---

[8] Sara Burrows, "85% of People Hate Their Jobs, Gallup Poll Says," September 22, 2017, returntonow.net

This service that you perform is not only supplying the needs of the Lord's people but is also overflowing in many expressions of thanks to God.

Because of the service by which you have proved yourselves, others will praise God for the obedience that accompanies your confession of the gospel of Christ, and for your generosity in sharing with them and with everyone else.

And in their prayers for you their hearts will go out to you, because of <u>the surpassing grace God has given you</u>. Thanks be to God for his indescribable gift!

—2 Corinthians 9:12-15

Let's stay focused on that answer—the grace of God, the empowerment to prosper!

Let's also be aware that the enemy wants you to stay in debt and never learn the way out. That is why there are 1.1 *trillion* active credit cards in the U.S.[9] It is also the reason four to eight billion credit card *offers* are sent out every year.[10]

Someone wants you in debt, and it is not just the banks and retailers who are begging you to try their cards.

Satan knows if he can keep you in debt, you will never be able to walk in your spiritual destiny, which he knows would wreak havoc in his kingdom.

So, let me review for a minute. This book is about being generous, right? Well, yes and no. Yes, we are going to talk about all the benefits of giving and being generous in a bit. But giving by itself is not the answer. You have to have the knowledge of how to tap into the grace,

---

[9] Raynor de Best, "Credit Card and Debit Card Number in the U.S. 2012-2018," December 16, 2020, statisa.com/statistics

[10] Bob Bryan, November 24, 2015, businessinsider.com

the power of God.

So, let me state again: The formula of giving by itself, just as a formula, is not the key. It is part of it, of course, but you and I need that supernatural, extraordinary empowerment to prosper called grace.

Dustin and Kendall discovered what I am talking about. They are a young couple who did not really understand they needed the grace of God in their finances until they found themselves in a mess. They had just looked at a new business idea and decided to move on it. The cost? $150,000, and all of it debt.

The same month they bought the business, they were audited by the IRS and were billed for $53,000 in back taxes. Dustin says they found themselves in over $200,000 of debt with really no way out, especially since things were already tight financially before they bought the business.

They had just borrowed the money to pay the hospital for their last baby and were making payments on that. The audit pushed them over the financial edge, and Dustin scrambled to find options.

After searching, he finally found an offer for a $30,000 line of credit, was approved, and took this idea to his wife for her opinion. What he did not know was that Kendall had been studying and meditating on my book, *Your Financial Revolution: The Power of Rest*, which also talks about tapping into the grace of God.

So when Dustin came to her with this loan idea, Kendall was disappointed, hoping he would turn to God instead of debt. She decided to talk to him about their decision and encouraged him to trust God. Graciously, Dustin received the wisdom of his wife.

As they prayed, they heard the Holy Spirit say to sow a seed. Of course, at the time, they did not have the money for the amount that God had shown them to give, so they worked for the next 28 days to earn enough to sow what God had shown them.

The result? Their business took off.

Over the next year, they were able to pay off $175,000 in debt, and Dustin said he made TWELVE times more money that year than he had ever made in his entire life!

Kendall and Dustin found out the Kingdom works every time!

What was their answer? The Kingdom and the grace of God!

What is your answer? The Kingdom and the grace of God!

CHAPTER 2
THE ANSWER: GRACE

In the last chapter, we talked about how generosity impacts people spiritually—how it softens their hearts with gratitude toward you and toward God. We also brought out what Paul said, that this ability to be generous was a result of the grace of God in our lives.

> *And in their prayers for you their hearts will go out to you, because of the surpassing grace God has given you. Thanks be to God for his indescribable gift!*
> —2 Corinthians 9:14-15

We talked about the emphasis Paul put on the word *surpassing* when he described the grace that God has given us to prosper. We found out that grace means an extraordinary empowerment to accomplish something. Paul calls this empowerment of God's grace an indescribable gift! I think anyone would have to admit that if God, Himself was going to help them prosper in life, that would be an incredible advantage.

To help you grasp the magnitude of what God wants to do in your life and the immense power available to you, let's back up a few verses and begin to read at verse six.

This is what I mean: The one who sows sparingly will also reap sparingly. The one who sows generously will also reap generously. Each one should give as he has determined in his heart, not reluctantly or under pressure, for God loves a cheerful giver. God is able to make all grace overflow to you, so that in all things, at all times, having all that you need, you will overflow in every good work. As it is written: He scattered; he gave to the poor. His righteousness remains forever.

And he who provides seed to the sower and bread for food will provide and multiply your seed for sowing, and will increase the harvest of righteousness. You will be made rich in every way so that you may be generous in every way, which produces thanksgiving to God through us.

—2 Corinthians 9:6-11 (EHV)

Now, here is where things get really exciting!

We see that same word *grace* used here, except in this passage Paul adds the adjective *all* to help the reader understand that ALL of God's power is behind that word grace. Paul is clearly talking about giving and receiving here and makes the point that once you give, all of God's grace is available to bring in the harvest.

All of God's grace implies that all of God's power, His wisdom, favor, and insight are now available to you to capture the harvest on that seed. I do not know about you, but that gets me excited!

But that still does not mean the harvest is just going to happen all by itself.

If a very wealthy farmer told you that he was going to lend you all of his farming equipment, worth millions of dollars, to plant and harvest a crop, but you knew nothing about farming, it would not profit you a thing.

God has made all of His power available to us, but we still have a part to play, just like a farmer knows there is a lot more to farming than just throwing seed into the ground.

For now, all I want you to understand is that all of God's ability is standing by not only to help you harvest after you sow but also even to help you know when and where to sow. And because of that, you have an unlimited financial future!!!!

YOU TAKE CARE OF GOD'S BUSINESS, AND HE WILL TAKE CARE OF YOURS.

Now, we need to go a step further and talk about the clear revelation in this passage as to the purpose of having money in the first place.

> *God is able to make all grace overflow to you, so that in all things, at all times, having all that you need, you will overflow in every good work.*

We see the first thing God mentions is having all that you need. Notice it is not just about money. He says in *all* things and at *all* times!

I always say it this way, "You take care of God's business, and He will take care of yours." So, "in all things and at all times" would mean to me that you would never go without, no matter what is happening in the economy. When God says your needs will be met, He is not talking about just getting by either.

> *You will lend to many nations but will borrow from none. The Lord will make you the head, not the tail. If you pay attention to the commands of the Lord your God that I give you this day and carefully follow them, you will always be at the top, never at the bottom.*
>
> —Deuteronomy 28:12b-13

When God is talking about all your needs being met, He is talking about walking in a place of total financial freedom with no debt, walking in your assignment with passion, and eating the best of the land. It also means you are in perfect health and have perfect peace.

Secondly, after your needs are met, you are not just surviving but thriving,

> *You will be made rich in every way so that <u>you may be generous in every way</u>.*

The end result is to have the financial ability to be generous, to give and support people, and to support God's assignments on the earth.

God's objective is to make His heart known to people and to move people's hearts toward Him.

As I always say, "God is in the people business."

Let me take a moment to address a false assumption that I hear so often.

I was talking to a very wealthy person the other day, and they said, "I do not need more money; I have plenty."

Now, I know what they were trying to say—that they are very well taken care of, and they do not need more money personally. But the fact is they do need more money and lots of it.

If we only look at what money can do for us *personally*, then I suppose there is a place where the drive to obtain more money could diminish. But if you understand God's heart to reach out to people and the millions who have yet to discover the good life there is in the Kingdom—but yet are headed at this moment to a real place called hell—then you would understand that God needs more money!!!!

Let me say that again, "**GOD NEEDS MORE MONEY!**"

There is still a lot of work to be done.

> And God is able to make all grace overflow to you, so that in all things, at all times, having all that you need, <u>you will overflow in every good work</u>.

You have every good work to attend to. Every good work is work done on behalf of the King. In fact, you have very specific work to do, according to Ephesians 4:7, 11-12a.

> But to each one of us grace has been given as Christ apportioned it. So Christ himself gave the apostles, the prophets, the evangelists, the pastors and teachers, to equip his people for <u>works of service</u>.
>
> —Ephesians 4:7, 11-12a

You see, most people aim at being financially free because they are tired of the rat race. They are looking for peace. And since most work in jobs they really do not like, they are looking for the freedom having money will give them. They are looking for the freedom to do what they *want* to do instead of what they *have* to do. They want to follow their passion and find the purpose their lives were meant to have.

Here is a statement that drives the religious people crazy:

You will be made rich in every way.

Yes, it does say that. You will be made rich!

Now the term rich is subjective, of course, and is mostly misunderstood in our culture. We really cannot say that someone who has one billion dollars is any happier than someone with $100,000. No, being "rich" means different things to different people. But, of course, it implies that all of our needs are met, that we're living debt free, and enjoying the best of the land.

If you are willing and obedient, you shall eat the good of the land.
—Isaiah 1:19

SO AGAIN, GOD WANTS YOU TO HAVE PLENTY OF PROVISION TO CARRY ON HIS WORK IN THE WORLD.

But being rich is not just about money. It is also about playing with my grandkids, holding hands with my wife, and so many other wonderful things in life. Drenda and I have five great kids, all who love God and in some way or another are involved in ministry. We all live close to each other, and, quite frankly, we love hanging out with each other. I call that rich!

You see, the religious folks think that having a lot of money is greed. But you cannot have too much money if you are in the people business with God. There are always new assignments and new territories to take.

So again, God wants you to have plenty of provision to carry on His work in the world.

God wants you to be generous for Him, helping people, and funding His assignments. If you are going to be able to be generous on every occasion, you must have some money.

I mean, every occasion could be *every day* or *multiple times a day*. Let's be honest—to be able to do that, you would not be living month to month; you would have more money than what was needed to pay your bills, a lot more! I think everyone would agree with that.

But let's get down to where the rubber meets the road when we talk about being generous or giving in general:

You have to deal with fear when you give.

I did not say you have to *put up* with fear. I said you have to DEAL with fear when you give. And the best way to deal with fear is with truth!

So what is the fear in giving? Simply put, it is that we will not have enough for ourselves, right?

I need that money, you may think, and of course you need it. But God needs it also. And God is not going to ask you to give Him your money to use without a promise back to you, a return on your investment so to speak, is He? I think He makes it pretty clear in His Word:

> *Give, and it will be given to you. A good measure, pressed down, shaken together and running over, will be poured into your lap.*
>
> —Luke 6:38a

God spends more time explaining to you the benefit of supporting His Kingdom than He does instructing you on what to do. He simply says one word, "*Give,*" but uses 23 words to explain *the benefit* to you. I think I would sign any contract constructed like that!

Know that God has a vested interest in you doing well. Think about it: Where is God going to get the money He needs to fund His agenda?

That money is going to have to come from you, me, and other fellow believers, of course. Satan's people are not going to fund God's assignments.

The sad thing is that the majority of believers would say it is wrong to believe God for a return on their giving. They believe giving to God and expecting anything back would be based on greed and diminish the pure act of worshiping God.

Do you believe a farmer is off base to believe his giving will produce a profit for him and his family? He is simply using the laws that God gave him.

God delights in seeing us prosper. He gave us the law of sowing and reaping for our benefit. The devil has lied to the church about giving and money since the beginning of time. Some denominations take pride in their vows of poverty, not realizing they are falling straight into Satan's lies. Jesus had to deal with that attitude many times in His ministry. In fact, He told one of his most famous parables regarding this very issue, the parable of the Good Samaritan.

> *On one occasion an expert in the law stood up to test Jesus. "Teacher," he asked, "what must I do to inherit eternal life?"*
>
> *"What is written in the Law?" he replied. "How do you read it?"*
>
> *He answered, "Love the Lord your God with all your heart and with all your soul and with all your strength and with all your mind"; and, "Love your neighbor as yourself."*
>
> *"You have answered correctly," Jesus replied. "Do this and you will live."*
>
> *But he wanted to justify himself, so he asked Jesus, "And who is my neighbor?"*
>
> *In reply Jesus said: "A man was going down from Jerusalem to Jericho, when he was attacked by robbers. They stripped him of his clothes, beat him and went away, leaving him half dead. A priest happened to be going down the same road, and when he saw the man, he passed by on the other side. So too, a Levite, when he came to the place and saw him, passed by on the other*

side. But a Samaritan, as he traveled, came where the man was; and when he saw him, he took pity on him. He went to him and bandaged his wounds, pouring on oil and wine. Then he put the man on his own donkey, brought him to an inn and took care of him. The next day he took out two denarii and gave them to the innkeeper. 'Look after him,' he said, 'and when I return, I will reimburse you for any extra expense you may have.'"

"Which of these three do you think was a neighbor to the man who fell into the hands of robbers?"

The expert in the law replied, "The one who had mercy on him."

Jesus told him, "Go and do likewise."

—Luke 10:25-37

I think all of us have heard this story with the lesson being: What would God do if He were walking down the road and saw this guy? We know the Lord would not leave this beaten man there to die along the road.

The lesson that most Sunday school classes teach from this is to be a good neighbor. Take care of people. Taking care of people is God's heart, and I can say I agree one hundred percent with that assessment. However, there is a whole lot more that is often left out.

To truly understand Jesus's rebuke toward this teacher of the law, you need to understand the social climate of the day. The Jews despised the Samaritans and considered them to be unclean and unspiritual. Thus, the Jews viewed themselves as much more holy and righteous in God's eyes than the Samaritans to the degree they would not even associate with them. So Jesus's story is basically a slap in the face to this teacher of the law, a rebuke for his pious attitude. I think we all get that understanding.

But the part I have never heard, and I mean have never heard taught in any Sunday school class ever, is the part of the story involving the two silver coins. Why did Jesus talk about the two silver coins if His point was already made concerning this teacher's wrong heart toward the Samaritans? Let's find out.

> *Then he put the man on his own donkey, brought him to an inn and took care of him. The next day he took out two denarii and gave them to the innkeeper. "Look after him," he said, "and when I return, I will reimburse you for any extra expense you may have."*
>
> —Luke 10:34a-35

In this story that Jesus is teaching, we can also see that it is an analogy of what Jesus was about to do for us. We can see mankind battered and bruised by Satan, the thief. We understand the oil and wine are prophetically representing the Holy Spirit and the blood covenant which Jesus will give to all who come to Him. And we see in the story that, after applying the oil and wine, the Samaritan goes a step further and moves this injured man to an inn to heal. The Samaritan knows the man needs time to heal, and he takes him to a safe place to recover, all at his expense.

I believe the inn represents the local church. This is where Jesus brings the people who have been found battered and dying along life's road. They are born again, having been cleansed from sin by the blood covenant and made alive by the Holy Spirit, yet they still carry with them the stain and pain of the earth curse system. They need time to heal and to learn a completely new way of living. Jesus sets them in a local church and under an innkeeper, the local pastor, to oversee their progress.

But unfortunately, we find the same attitude in the church that the teacher of the law had. People do not want to get involved in helping out at the inn. Like those who passed the injured man by, they viewed his problem as someone else's problem. Why should they get involved? What was in it for them except costing them time and money?

Because of this attitude, pastors spend much of their time begging people to help out in the nursery or to help lead a small group. But it seems people are already busy doing their own thing and find it hard to commit. Religion itself offers no incentive, only duty and law. Religion tries to guilt people into helping by saying, "You owe it to God to take care of this or that. After all, look what God has done for you." And I agree, we should always have willing and grateful hearts toward God and have a desire to help others, but God does not operate with the "You owe me" system. He says, "I am leaving you two coins to cover expenses and will pay you WHATEVER it costs you when I return."

Again, the religious mindset will take that statement as meaning when we get to heaven, Jesus will reward us for the work we have done here on the earth for His Kingdom. No, when Jesus was telling the story, He was referring to when the businessman would be passing by on his return trip to town. Jesus was talking about real-time financial help for that innkeeper. But people will now say, "Great, God is going to cover the inn's expense while taking care of this person, but I also have real expenses here at my house. I cannot afford the time or the money to get involved." This mindset of simply being reimbursed for any expense you may incur for getting involved does not motivate many people. It helps, of course, but it does not reveal the whole story of God's love for those who do get involved.

Yes, I know what you will say: "We should all help out at the inn simply out of our love for God." Yes, you could do it out of your loyalty to your pastor and your love and duty toward God, and that is required sometimes… But God wants you to be *excited* to "work at the inn" with Him.

And that is the point—we are not working FOR God but, rather, WITH God. God, Himself says the following through Paul:

> *Who serves as a soldier at his own expense? Who plants a vineyard and does not eat its grapes? Who tends a flock and does not drink the milk? Do I say this merely on human authority? Doesn't the Law say the same thing? For it is written in the Law of Moses: "Do not muzzle an ox while it is treading out the grain." Is it about oxen that God is concerned? Surely, he says this for us, doesn't he? Yes, this was written for us, because whoever plows and threshes should be able to do so in the hope of sharing in the harvest.*
>
> —1 Corinthians 9:7-10

God does not want you to serve Him out of fear or simple duty.

Notice what He said, "*Whoever plows and threshes should be able to do so in the hope of sharing in the harvest.*" God does not just care for the harvest that is a result of the assignment He has you on. He also cares for those who are working right there alongside Him, and He wants them to share in the joy of the harvest just as He does.

Jesus chose an innkeeper for the story for a very important reason. We understand that the innkeeper is operating a business. He has built into his daily rate the price for overhead and staff. But on top of all the expenses needed to run the inn, he adds profit. That's right, *profit.*

Every time the innkeeper charges his guest for a night's stay, he makes a profit. Because of this, the innkeeper has a very different perspective toward the injured man that was brought to his door. It is not costing him a cent to take care of him, as the traveler has promised to cover his expenses. But the innkeeper knows a fact that allows him to help this man without a grudge. In fact, he is almost giddy over the opportunity that he finds himself in.

You see, the innkeeper understands that each night the man stays there, he will make a profit, and with an open checkbook offered by the traveling businessman, he is ecstatic. I can just imagine the innkeeper's conversation with the traveling businessman as he leaves on his journey: "Hey, if you see anyone else that needs help along the road, be sure to bring them here. I will take all you can bring me, and if I run out of room, I will add on!"

As you can see, there is a whole lot more to the story than just the familiar story of what would Jesus do. Jesus was trying to correct the religious mindset that the expert in the law had toward God and the Samaritan. He was also making

THEY SADLY MISS GOD'S HEART, THAT HE IS WILLING TO PAY WHATEVER IT COSTS TO REACH PEOPLE, AND HE ALWAYS GIVES US MORE THAN WE INVEST. ALWAYS.

a point to let him know that he was missing out on a tremendous opportunity that the Samaritan had captured—*profit*!

I am always sad when I hear people say that God does bad things to good people, or I see people serving God out of a religious duty instead of the exciting life they could have. Satan has tried to hide God's goodness from God's people so that they would not willingly serve Him with their whole hearts.

To most people, church is just another event on the calendar instead of understanding that they are the church, the inn where God sends people to become whole. They sadly miss God's heart, that He is willing to pay whatever it costs to reach people, and He always gives us more than we invest. Always.

I can remember sitting down with Drenda's brother years ago discussing this very point—that God is good and a rewarder, and He has given us the Kingdom that meets all our needs. This understanding of the Kingdom was new to Johnny and his wife, Candi, as they had come out of a traditional church where little truth was taught.

Johnny and Candi were teachers in the Georgia school system at the time, and while teaching, Johnny worked part time with my financial company, Forward Financial Group. It seemed that Johnny was a natural in the business. In his first year with the company, he made more part time than he did in a year of teaching, so he decided to quit teaching and go full time in the financial business.

At first, Johnny did very well. But later in that year, I saw that his activity began to slow, and I knew that he could not continue at that pace for long.

Drenda and I had planned a trip to Georgia for the Christmas season, and it was my full intention to stop and spend some time with Johnny to see if I could identify some of the reasons that he was not producing the business he needed to stay full time. Before I could call Johnny, he called me and asked if I could stop over to discuss business. Of course, I was already prepared to do just that.

I could tell that Johnny and Candi were scared. They already had $5,000 worth of bills due for the current month, and they had no money set to come in for the next month's $5,000 they would need. As I sat down with Johnny, his first words were, "It is just not working." I knew that the Kingdom understanding was all new to Johnny and Candi, and I felt that I needed to coach them on how to handle this spiritually. Because I knew the Kingdom always works! So I spent about two hours with them going over the laws of the

Kingdom and how to release their faith. As I spoke, I could sense fear fading and faith beginning to rise. I knew Johnny was ready for the next step.

"Johnny," I said, "You need to plant a seed with God and believe Him for the money you need."

Johnny and Candi agreed, but they had no money. It just so happened that I had brought with me a paycheck for $160 for Johnny from the home office. I knew they could use that money, but I encouraged them instead to sow it as a seed as we both knew that the $160, by itself, could not take care of the $5,000 in bills they needed to catch up on or the $5,000 in bills that were coming due. They agreed.

As we were about to pray and release our faith together, I asked Johnny, "What are you believing to receive as you sow this money?" As the words left my mouth, the Holy Spirit stopped me and said not to let him answer, and I knew why. Johnny would have said he believed for the $5,000, because obviously, that was where the pressure was. Instead, the Holy Spirit said to me, "Ask him if $12,000 in 30 days would be enough."

So, I did just that. I stopped him from answering and asked him if $12,000 in 30 days would be enough. I could see his eyes open wide as I stated the amount the Lord told me to ask him. I knew that Johnny had never made $12,000 in 30 days in his entire life. He sat there for a minute and then said, yes, he could believe that with me. I asked Candi the same question, and she said yes as well. We joined hands, laid them on that check, and released our faith for $12,000 in 30 days.

Three weeks later, I received a call from Johnny. Boy, was he excited. He had written enough business in the past three weeks to pay him not just $12,000 but $17,000. He said he was really a believer now.

Unfortunately, two months later, Johnny lost control of his car on a rainy night heading home after an appointment. The car was totaled, but Johnny lived through the crash, which in itself was an act of God. However, due to the accident, Johnny was unable to work as he recovered. During that time period, his house fell into foreclosure and was set for a sheriff's sale. He needed $10,000 to pull the house out of the sale.

During this time, however, Johnny and Candi had decided that they needed to move to Ohio to get closer to the Kingdom teaching that was changing their lives. So, they listed the house, even though they knew they only had about one month before the sheriff's sale was to occur.

As the date drew closer, no real buyers came by until just a few days before the sale when a man stopped by and offered to buy the house. But he had a request. He wanted to know if he gave Johnny $10,000 now, could he hold the house for 30 days until he finished up some other business which was going to fund the purchase.

Johnny was shocked. He knew that if he was going to pull the house out of the sheriff's sale, it had to be a cash buyer as the sale was only a couple of days away. This buyer wanted to write Johnny a $10,000 check on the spot and then close later. This was the exact amount that Johnny needed. Johnny knew it was God, took the $10,000 check, and paid the house to current. Oh, and that $10,000 was money *on top of* the list price.

So Johnny and Candi moved to Ohio and settled into a rented home. They got involved with Faith Life Church, and Johnny jumped into the financial business with renewed vigor. But now they had a new problem. They only had one car, and Johnny needed it to cover the many appointments he had during the week meeting clients. Well, they knew what to do. They sowed a seed for a new car and believed they received it when they prayed, according to Mark 11:24.

Then the most unusual thing happened. A childhood friend of Johnny's called…

"Johnny, did I ever pay you back for that bicycle you gave me in sixth grade?" he asked.

"No," Johnny said.

Then his friend said, "Well, I am going to pay you back now. I am going to buy you a BMW."

As kids, the two boys always talked about cars, and he knew that Johnny had always wanted a BMW. The friend was true to his word and wired Johnny the money to buy himself a BMW. But once Johnny got the money, he realized that with a growing family, a BMW was not the car he really needed. He and Candi decided to get Candi a family SUV and a smaller car for Johnny's business driving since Candi's small car they were driving was old and had problems. So that is what happened.

I can remember the night that Johnny called me. He was sitting in his new SUV in his driveway next to his other new car with tears in his eyes as he told me how shocked he was to have two paid for cars for the first time in his life.

Johnny was a new person. He knew then that God could do anything.

One day he came by my office and said that he was tired of renting a house, that he and Candi wanted a farm with land and they were looking. Well, I knew that Johnny's credit was not good due to the wreck and encouraged him to just rent a bit longer and build his cash reserve to allow time for his credit score to rise. But Johnny did not seem to pay much attention to what I said.

He then told me that he had seen a farm down the street from me that was for sale, and he was going to check into buying it. Of course, since I owned a mortgage company at the time, I knew there was no way that Johnny would be able to qualify for that farm. I also knew he did not have the down payment for such a purchase.

I was shocked a week later when he walked back into my office with a grin and said the farm was his. When he told me that, I knew that was a story I had to hear. Of course, he and Candi had sown a financial seed into the work of God as they had been taught to believe they had received when they prayed. Then Johnny went on and explained to me what had happened.

He went to see his bank about the purchase, and the manager pulled his credit report and sat down with him and told him, "Johnny, you were right about your credit. You do not qualify to buy anything."

But then the manager said something strange. He pushed the credit file to the side and said, "But I like you. Let me see what I can do."

To make a long story a little shorter, the bank financed 100% of the purchase, gave him four months until the lease he had at the time ran out to move in, filled the propane tank, paid the outstanding property taxes, and gave Johnny a $5,000 check at closing to fix the crack in the concrete of the front porch.

I sat there stunned as Johnny just kept going on and on about the Kingdom. "Wow!" was all I could say.

A month later, Johnny told me that he had sown a seed for a Ford tractor. He told me that he decided he needed a tractor on his new farm and had sown a very specific seed for a blue diesel Ford tractor. Again, since he worked for me, and knowing the price of tractors, I knew that he did not yet have that kind of money.

But sure enough, a few weeks later as I looked toward the road, I saw Johnny driving a blue Ford diesel tractor toward his house. When I asked him where and how he got the tractor, he said a woman randomly walked up to him at church and asked him if he knew anyone that might need a tractor. They were liquidating her parents' farm, and there was this tractor they were trying to get rid of. Johnny told her he was interested.

Well, she told him not to worry about paying her, just to pay when he could; she was in no hurry. So then he had his tractor.

His success continued. The next month, he made $72,000 in just one month. If you asked Johnny how that happened, he would say it happened by being generous toward God and understanding the laws of the Kingdom.

What a story! I can still remember sitting down with Johnny and Candi in their Georgia home that night sharing the Kingdom with them. They were overwhelmed with being $5,000 behind on their bills and facing Christmas and another round of $5,000 worth of bills coming up with no money in sight. I thought you might be interested in hearing what I said to them that night.

I knew that I simply had to help them see God through the haze of the circumstances that faced them. I began by showing them what we have been talking about in 2 Corinthians 9:10-11:

> *Now he who supplies seed to the sower and bread for food will also supply and increase your store of seed and will enlarge the harvest of your righteousness. You will be enriched in every way so that you can be generous on every occasion, and through us your generosity will result in thanksgiving to God.*

I pointed out that Paul was saying that God is not only going to supply the seed you sow but also that He will provide the bread for your own needs. Bread is referring to all that you need personally in your life. From that, He is going to increase your ability to give even more. That means you are going to increase.

Again, what is the fear in giving? That you will run short for your own needs.

But pay attention to what God says. He gives seed to the sower and bread for food. Now, here is a very important question, and this was the question I asked Johnny.

Is what you have in your hand seed or is it food? It is your choice.

My mom's dad, my grandpa, was a farmer all his life. I remember as a young boy playing in his seed wagon. You may have never heard of a seed wagon. It may not even be a real term, but it was to us growing up with Grandpa. You see, every year at harvest, Grandpa always kept back enough seed to fill a wagon he had in the barn. That wagon was full of the seed he was saving to plant in the spring for the next year's crop.

During the winter months, Grandpa had to look at that big wagon brimming full of soybeans, knowing he had a choice to sell it for an immediate need or save it for spring planting where he knew it would produce a big harvest. He had a choice, but he was convinced of the laws that governed seed time and harvest, and he staked his life on them.

Johnny and Candi had to face that same decision when holding that $160 check. They sure could have used it to pay a pressing need, but instead, they knew that being generous toward God would give them a bigger harvest in the long run. And they were correct.

One person gives freely, yet gains even more; another

withholds unduly, but comes to poverty.

—Proverbs 11:24

Before we close out this chapter, there is one more parable I would like to look at—Matthew 25:14-30, the parable of the talents.

Again, it will be like a man going on a journey, who called his servants and entrusted his wealth to them. To one he gave five bags of gold, to another two bags, and to another one bag, each according to his ability. Then he went on his journey. The man who had received five bags of gold went at once and put his money to work and gained five bags more. So also, the one with two bags of gold gained two more. But the man who had received one bag went off, dug a hole in the ground and hid his master's money.

After a long time the master of those servants returned and settled accounts with them. The man who had received five bags of gold brought the other five. "Master," he said, "you entrusted me with five bags of gold. See, I have gained five more."

His master replied, "Well done, good and faithful servant! You have been faithful with a few things; I will put you in charge of many things. Come and share your master's happiness!"

The man with two bags of gold also came. "Master," he said, "you entrusted me with two bags of gold; see, I have gained two more."

His master replied, "Well done, good and faithful servant! You have been faithful with a few things; I will put you in charge of many things. Come and share your master's happiness!"

Then the man who had received one bag of gold came. "Master," he said, "I knew that you are a hard man, harvesting where you have not sown and gathering where you have not scattered seed. So I was afraid and went out and hid your gold in the ground. See, here is what belongs to you."

His master replied, "You wicked, lazy servant! So you knew that I harvest where I have not sown and gather where I have not scattered seed? Well then, you should have put my money on deposit with the bankers, so that when I returned I would have received it back with interest."

So take the bag of gold from him and give it to the one who has ten bags. For whoever has will be given more, and they will have an abundance. Whoever does not have, even what they have will be taken from them. And throw that worthless servant outside, into the darkness, where there will be weeping and gnashing of teeth.

—Matthew 25:14-30

The story is a familiar one. The master is leaving town and leaves three servants in charge. To one he gives five bags of gold, to one he gives two bags of gold, and to one he gives one bag of gold.

The first two go to work immediately and double the bags of gold they have. The master applauds them for their work. But it is the third servant that I want to look at. He was given one bag of gold but did nothing with it. In fact, he just buried it until his master came back.

Then the man who had received one bag of gold came. "Master," he said, "I knew that you are a hard man, harvesting where you have not sown and gathering where you have not scattered seed. So I was afraid and went out and hid your gold in the ground. See, here is what belongs to you."

Pay close attention to the first sentence: "*Master, I knew that you were a hard man, harvesting where you have not sown and gathering where you have not scattered seed.*"

What is he saying? I will tell you exactly what he is saying. He's saying, "Why should I get involved? If you are harvesting where you have not planted seed, then who paid for the seed and who scattered it and did all the work growing it?"

Now, we understand that the master gave him the money to buy the seed, but his attitude was that it was not worth his time to get involved. There was nothing in it for him. All the profit, the result of his work, was going to the master. Because of his image of the master, who he saw as a hard taskmaster, he basically refused to get involved. He tried to hide his true contempt for the master by stating his motive to hide the money was because he was afraid of losing it, and so he had hidden the gold to protect it. But the master called his bluff and said that if he really cared for him, he would have at least put the money on deposit at the bank, and there, it would have gained interest.

No, the servant was not afraid of losing the gold; he was afraid of what it would cost him to get involved. He had a perverse and wicked image of the master, perverse because the opposite was actually true. The master was not a hard taskmaster. The other two servants were rewarded with promotion and invited to enjoy the master's estate after they successfully worked with the master's money. This servant, because of his wrong image of the master, chose not to participate. And this is exactly what religion teaches us—that God is a hard taskmaster and there is no profit in working with Him, so why get involved?

But that image of God is totally perverse and not true. To call God unfair is wicked. God is exactly the opposite of that portrayal.

He is good and a rewarder.

But now I want to emphasize a very important point that is made in this story. Pay close attention to what the master does with the gold that he takes back from the wicked servant.

> *So take the bag of gold from him and give it to the one who has ten bags. For whoever has will be given more, and they will have an abundance. Whoever does not have, even what they have will be taken from them. And throw that worthless servant outside, into the darkness, where there will be weeping and gnashing of teeth.*

Did I read that right? The master took the bag of gold from the worthless servant and gave it to the one that had ten and not the one that had four? I am not sure that would be politically correct, but that is what he did. **PAY CAREFUL ATTENTION!!!!**

GOD IS GOING TO GIVE HIS GREAT IDEAS AND ASSIGNMENTS TO HIS CHILDREN WHO HAVE HIS PROFIT IN MIND...

God is going to give His great ideas and assignments to His children who have His profit in mind and have proven themselves loyal and faithful in the small jobs first.

God is not stupid. He is going to put His money where it will have the greatest return.

Please think about what I have just said—God is going to put His money where it will have the greatest return!

Now, of course, God is not in the *money* business, but He is in the *people* business. And as we are faithful to work diligently with Him, He will promote us and give us favor with His good things.

Yes, God has favorites in the sense of who He trusts with different assignments. Those who have proven themselves faithful will earn

God's trust to handle bigger and more rewarding assignments for him.

Notice the attitude of the two servants that were successful—they went at once and put their master's money to work! Why immediately? Because they knew this was an *opportunity,* not a weight of slavery.

So many of God's people view serving God as a drudgery, a duty to be fulfilled and not the opportunity that it really is.

When Drenda and I were building the Now Center campus, we had to make a decision. We were a church of only about 300 when we decided that we needed to build a permanent and bigger home for our growing body of believers.

We set out to raise as much money as we could toward what would be a $6 million project. This was a huge amount of money to us at the time. The plan was to build the basic infrastructure for about $4.2 million and then add the remaining $2 million worth of equipment and build out as the money came in.

This was not our first experience with being generous toward God's projects, but it was the biggest one we had been a part of up to that point.

However, like the servants in the story who knew God's goodness, we immediately wanted to be a part of raising the money, and we wanted to give at a level that would require faith and obedience to what we believed God was telling us.

On the day that the entire congregation declared what they had agreed on sowing into the project, Drenda and I said we were giving $200,000. Now, at the time, we did not have the $200,000, but we had seed of about $20,000 that we were going to sow for the remaining balance.

We knew, as He had in the past, that God would show us where and how to harvest that amount of money with plenty left over for ourselves.

After sowing what we had, we began to pray in the Spirit, waiting for direction and instruction as to where and how to capture the remaining amount of money. To set the stage so you will understand how God brought this money in, I need to tell you that we have owned a financial company for the last 39 years. That company works with various vendors and professionals, as I mentioned to you earlier. Most of the bigger vendors we work with have annual conventions and get-togethers for their clients.

In this particular year, one of our vendors had invited Drenda and me to come to London, England, for their convention. We were staying at a very nice hotel in downtown London, and it was just lovely, as they say in London.

Well, the company had one event that was on the other side of town, and the vice president invited Drenda and me to ride with her in a cab to the event, which we gladly accepted. During the taxi ride, the vice president thanked us for all the business we had sent them and then began telling us about a new bonus program they were launching that year.

She went on to explain how it worked and the bonus structure that they were going to pay out to the associates who recommended their product. I was very excited as she spoke, as I knew we did enough business to qualify for the bonus she was talking about.

Then, just as I asked for further details, she abruptly stated that our company would not qualify for the bonus program based on the structure of our relationship with her company.

I could not believe it. Why did she go through all the detail and sell me on this great plan to simply take it away from me at the last minute? I also did not understand how my relationship to her company was structured so as not to be able to qualify for the bonus.

Even though I asked further questions, she did not really give me a clear answer. The only thing I knew for sure was that I would not be able to qualify for the bonus; she made that clear.

A year went by and our production was good for that year, so I had the thought to call her up and again inquire about the bonus. However, this time when I called, I could not reach her, so I left a message with her assistant with my question.

The next day, her assistant called me back, and with a stern sounding voice, stated that the vice president had already told me a year earlier that I did not qualify, and there was nothing she could do about it.

Well, okay, I thought, *at least I tried.*

YOU SEE, GOD IS A REWARDER! AND THERE IS PROFIT IN BEING GENEROUS TOWARD GOD'S ASSIGNMENTS.

Now, as I was praying about where to find the $180,000, I heard the Holy Spirit tell me to call the vice president and ask for that bonus again. I will tell you that I was not thrilled to hear that. After my experience asking her the last two years, I knew where she stood. She had made that very clear. So, I thought I would just send her an email to just test the waters, so to speak.

About seven days later I received her reply, which to my joy said she had thought about it and had decided to give my company the bonus. Amazingly, the bonus was $200,000! Now, here is the best part. That contract change has stayed in place now for the last 14 YEARS, and we have received that $200,000 bonus every year since.

You see, God is a rewarder! And there is profit in being generous toward God's assignments.

So how much did it cost Drenda and me to sow that $200,000?

About five years went by, and we decided that as a church we needed to raise more money to complete a few things at church and buy some equipment. Again, Drenda and I had to decide how much we wanted to sow toward those projects, and we decided on $500,000.

Wow, that was a lot of money. But we felt we could trust God with it after seeing what He did with the $200,000. Again, we sowed what we could, which I think was $50,000, and were believing for the Holy Spirit to show us where and how to capture the remaining $450,000.

I think maybe six weeks went by, and I received a notice that there was going to be a few contractual changes on how we were to be paid in our company. After we calculated the changes that were taking place, we would make about $630,000 more over the next three years than we had been making. Pretty cool, right? Well, guess what? That contractual change has stayed in place now for the last 11 years, and we still get that increased contract rate every year.

Again, how much did it cost Drenda and me to sow and be generous toward God's projects?

So remember that God is a God of profit. He is good and a rewarder.

CHAPTER 3
DO YOU QUALIFY?

I think everyone has heard the Christmas story and about the three kings that brought Jesus gold, frankincense, and myrrh. Have you ever wondered what those items were worth? A better question is, "Why did they bring it to Him in the first place?"

Well, with some investigation, I found out that it was common in those days to honor a prince with these types of gifts, as He was seen as the future king.

The best estimate is that these gifts were probably worth between $100,000 and hundreds of thousands of dollars.

The wise men must have studied the Scriptures and prophecies concerning the coming Messiah, and upon seeing the star concluded that He was there, then traveled a great distance to bring Him gifts.

The concept that they met Jesus at the manger is not what happened, even though it is portrayed that way in our Christmas plays. We know this because Matthew says the following.

> On coming <u>to the house</u>, they saw the child with his mother Mary, and they bowed down and worshiped him. Then they opened their treasures and presented him with gifts of gold, frankincense and myrrh.
>
> —Matthew 2:11

They met Jesus at His home, not at the manger. The passage indicates that He was a young child, not a baby. So it must have taken a while for the wise men to get there.

Second, no one really knows how many wise men there were. The Bible does not say how many came, but it does record what they brought. At that time, frankincense and myrrh were actually more valuable than gold, so the gifts they brought were extremely valuable.

So why do I bring this up? Well, let me ask you, "Why do you think these wise men brought these gifts?"

I can tell you why—Joseph needed provision for his assignment. Remember...

God always funds His assignments—always!

Faith Life Church was packed. It was packed on the weekends, packed during the week as we educated over 200 kids, packed with small groups and staff. We needed more room. We began to discuss whether we should open a second campus or build on to our current building. We decided to do both at the same time.

So, we assembled a team to begin looking for a campus site, and we directed them toward the area of town that we felt we should look at first.

Then, at the same time, we began the first steps in building design, engineering studies, and so forth in order to expand. We engaged an architect and a builder and put together an advisory board, all with contracting experience.

We discovered there were some serious issues with adding on. The biggest was that we had no sewer and no water to our present building. We were using well water and a self-contained waste management system for our sewer.

The county had already told us that we could not build on or add additional buildings to our 36-acre campus unless we had city water and sewer to the building, as we had maxed out the capacity that they would allow. We knew that going in, but there was so much new building going on around us that I felt for sure they must be close to bringing the water and sewer lines near enough to reach.

But we found out the water and sewer lines were not even on our street yet, so it was not a matter of simply tapping into those services. They just were not there.

We began to get bids on bringing the water and sewer lines to our building with us paying for it and then recouping much of the cost as new development paid us tap fees to tap into the lines. You do not want to know how much we found out that would cost.

So, we went back to the city and reviewed their plans and timeline for when these services would be available and hoped they would consider moving those dates up a bit since the area was growing and they would be needed eventually. But they did not budge. So how long did they say it would take before services would be available? Not anytime soon.

We knew that we could not wait years for the water and sewer lines to become available in our area, so we decided to put our addition on hold and began to look for a campus site as our primary objective. (It has been four years now from that meeting to the time of writing this chapter, and the city still has no word when the sewer line will be available.)

GOD ALWAYS FUNDS HIS ASSIGNMENTS— ALWAYS!

Well, our team searched for six months for the perfect campus site with no luck. It seemed that there were no buildings that fit our description available to rent or to buy. So, we considered renting an event center in the area, and just for the weekends, that was going to cost $30,000 a month. On top of the cost, we would have to set up and tear down each week. I really did not want to put our people in that situation. I wanted a permanent site that we could control. We did not have peace about the event center.

We then looked at leasing a space in a rundown strip mall. But after considering all of the repairs and changes that would be required to bring it up to code, we decided it was not really a go either.

One of our core values in finding a building was that it must be able to support children's education during the week. We have hundreds of homeschooling families in our church, and we host a co-op as well as classes each week. We have talked many times about someday possibly having a school, having a daycare center, an after school program, and many more programs to minister to our local communities. We wanted to find a space that would allow us to do just that. We had sown toward receiving that building, claiming we would find the perfect building for our needs, but it just was not showing up.

Drenda and I were scheduled to attend a meeting in Fort Worth, Texas, in support of the new Victory Television Network. While there, as I was sitting on the set, the Lord spoke to me. He said, "*I want you to sow $100,000 into this network. Go home to your church, make the check out, and hold it in each service and declare over that seed that you will find the perfect building. Also, rebuke Satan and tell him to stop interfering with My work. Call it done as you sow.*"

So that is what we did. We went home, and I called my treasurer and told him to make out a $100,000 check to the Victory Television Network. I then took that check to each service, and the whole church agreed with me as we sowed that seed for the perfect building. We rebuked Satan and told him to stop interfering and delaying our provision.

The next day, Monday morning, we received a call from our

daughter, who said that while we were at the meeting in Texas, the real estate agent had offered to show them an interesting piece of property. It was not for lease and was really not in our budget, as it was listed for sale for $7.9 million. But it was worth a lot more as it was a bank-owned foreclosure. She said it would be the perfect campus, but, of course, she knew it really was not an option financially. But she wanted to know if we wanted to see it anyway. We said sure.

So, Tuesday morning, we went to look at the property. The property was on seven acres and had been a high-end private high school campus. It had a three-story high school building and two more large buildings, as well as a house on the property. It had a running track, four tennis courts, weight rooms, an art building with a photo lab, two kilns for pottery making, a room full of sewing equipment and art supplies, dozens of musical instruments in the music room, and so much more. The whole property was fully furnished and stocked with supplies.

As we walked around the property, it was just perfect. But at the same time, we knew that we could not go into debt for it. We had about $3 million saved in our building fund, but that would still leave us borrowing almost $5 million.

That night, we had a dinner planned with one of our ministry partners. Now, this dinner had been planned and moved probably four times over the fall as we both were so busy, but this night the date was held.

As we talked, the gentleman began to ask me about the building project, and I told him of all the delays that we had come up against. He looked at me and said, "You know, I am not feeling it. I really think you should consider opening a campus instead." I told him we agreed and, in fact, had been looking for a building for six months with no success. However, we told him we had just looked at the perfect campus site that day, but that it was not for lease and was out of our price range.

He asked a few questions about it, then he looked at Drenda and said, "What if it was free?" Drenda did not answer as she thought he was joking. Then he said it again, "Drenda, I said what if it was free?"

She asked, "What do you mean?"

"I will write the check for it!" he said.

Drenda and I sat there stunned.

To make a long story short, he did pay for it. We then had to spend some money on refurbishing and changing the building to match our intended use. The result is the perfect campus. And the building is paid for!

I could not have planned out a more perfect campus for our needs. Everything about it is perfect. We had an appraisal done for our insurance company, and it came back at $11 million, including the contents.

Think about it: We now have an $11 million campus with 89,000 square feet of space paid for! Don't you just love stories like that?

As I said, God always funds His assignments. It is His ministry, not ours. We are just working alongside Him in the family business.

Now, let me tell you what happened to the husband and wife who funded the building for us. First of all, due to the write-off they could

THE KINGDOM WORKS EVERY TIME!

now take for their donation, their tax bill was reduced by more than they had paid for the building. How? The building had to go into their name for two years. Then they donated the building to the ministry at the then current appraised value.

This is a strategy you should be aware of if you are a pastor and need a building. So, the building ended up really being free to both of us with some wise tax planning on his side. But even that was not the amazing side of the story.

This partner was trying to buy another business in town that was up for sale at the time we looked at the property. Even though he was making a cash offer, his bid had to be approved by the owners of the franchise he was wanting to purchase, and, unfortunately, they came back and said they had offered it to someone else. He was so disappointed in their decision. He told me he just could not let it go; he just felt in his spirit that it was not over.

So when he sowed that money toward our building, he told me that he sowed it believing that the franchise owners would change their minds, as he was in the strongest financial position compared to the other offers, and he was paying cash.

Well, sure enough, after the transaction went through on our property, he received a call from the owners stating that the previous deal had fallen through and it was now his if he wanted it. He said yes, for sure, he wanted it.

Then a few weeks before he was to close on this new business property, he had a completely unexpected deal fall in his lap that produced all the money needed to pay cash for the business. He did not have to touch the cash he had previously set aside to purchase it at all. He told me it was like getting a free business.

Oh, by the way, once he purchased the business, it appraised for more than double what he paid for it. When he called me the day he closed on the property, he was so excited.

The Kingdom works every time!

This partner was generous toward God's assignments and obedient to follow through and look at what God did for both of us. We sowed into a new TV station, another one of God's mandates, and look at what happened for us.

Being generous toward God and God's people will open doors

you never even thought existed.

People ask me all the time, "Gary, if you could give me one major key today regarding Kingdom finances, what would it be?"

Well, there are a lot of things I would love to tell you for sure. But the following bit of advice will be priceless. So be sure to take notes on the following Kingdom principle.

If you get nothing more out of this book: Get this!

I want to take you to Luke 4 as I begin to unpack this mighty law of the Kingdom for you. I know the following text is a little longer than I would usually quote, but reading the entire passage will give you a flavor of what is going on and why Jesus answered the way He did.

> *He went to Nazareth, where he had been brought up, and on the Sabbath day he went into the synagogue, as was his custom. He stood up to read, and the scroll of the prophet Isaiah was handed to him. Unrolling it, he found the place where it is written:*
>
>> *"The Spirit of the Lord is on me, because he has anointed me to proclaim good news to the poor. He has sent me to proclaim freedom for the prisoners and recovery of sight for the blind, to set the oppressed free, to proclaim the year of the Lord's favor."*
>
> *Then he rolled up the scroll, gave it back to the attendant and sat down. The eyes of everyone in the synagogue were fastened on him. He began by saying to them, "Today this scripture is fulfilled in your hearing."*
>
> *All spoke well of him and were amazed at the gracious words*

that came from his lips. "Isn't this Joseph's son?" they asked.

Jesus said to them, "Surely you will quote this proverb to me: 'Physician, heal yourself!' And you will tell me, 'Do here in your hometown what we have heard that you did in Capernaum.'"

"Truly I tell you," he continued, "no prophet is accepted in his hometown. I assure you that there were many widows in Israel in Elijah's time, when the sky was shut for three and a half years and there was a severe famine throughout the land. <u>Yet Elijah was not sent to any of them</u>, but to a widow in Zarephath in the region of Sidon."

—Luke 4:16-26

This text occurs after Jesus has been tempted in the wilderness and then returns to His hometown where we pick up the story as written.

Because Jesus was raised in Nazareth, they were very familiar with Him and His family, and we can assume that He had read Scripture many times at the local synagogue. Now there is something you need to know about the text Jesus chose to read to them. He was reading from Isaiah 61:1-2, and He read down until it says, "***to proclaim the year of the Lord's favor***," then He stopped.

Now, the interesting thing about where He stopped is that it is in the middle of a sentence, so we know that He stopped at that exact spot for a reason.

The year of the Lord's favor was the year of Jubilee, and it represented the restoration of the Kingdom of God in the earth realm. It was a shadow of what the Messiah was going to restore when He came. So, when Jesus stopped on that phrase and then said, "***Today this scripture is fulfilled in your hearing***," He was declaring that He was the Messiah!

He then went on and prophesied what they would say to Him in the future, which was basically, "We do not believe you; prove it to us," because they did not believe Him.

> *Jesus said to them, "Surely you will quote this proverb to me: 'Physician, heal yourself!' And you will tell me, 'Do here in your hometown what we have heard that you did in Capernaum.'"*

Capernaum is where Jesus set up His ministry headquarters and where most of His miracles took place. He was prophesying to them that they would hear of great wonders that would occur in Capernaum, and when they heard of these things, they would be saying to come here and do the same works here in Nazareth so we can believe you. The fact is, He was convicting them of their hard hearts and unbelief. He knew they did not believe Him, and He knew they were never going to believe Him. We know that because He added that they would also say, *"Physician, heal yourself!"* in reference to what would be said at His crucifixion.

> *Those who passed by hurled insults at him, shaking their heads and saying, "You who are going to destroy the temple and build it in three days, save yourself! Come down from the cross, if you are the Son of God!" In the same way the chief priests, the teachers of the law and the elders mocked him. "He saved others," they said, "but he can't save himself! He's the king of Israel! Let him come down now from the cross, and we will believe in him."*
> —Matthew 27:39-42

From the beginning of His ministry to the end, He was saying that in spite of all they would hear, they would not receive His message. He then went on to make His message to them clearer by telling the story of Elijah and the widow, where God had to send Elijah outside of Israel because the people of Israel had such hard hearts and could not believe. This infuriated the teachers of the law to the point that they took Jesus outside to kill Him, but the Bible says He slipped away.

Now I want you to write down a word for me and put it somewhere where you can remember it, because it is key to your financial future. Write down the word "SENT." That's right, the word "SENT." This is very important!

<u>SENT</u>

I want to go to 1 Kings 17:7-16 where we will find a mystery so powerful that it will absolutely change your life.

> *Some time later the brook dried up because there had been no rain in the land. Then the word of the Lord came to him: "Go at once to Zarephath in the region of Sidon and stay there. I have directed a widow there to supply you with food." So he went to Zarephath. When he came to the town gate, a widow was there gathering sticks. He called to her and asked, "Would you bring me a little water in a jar so I may have a drink?" As she was going to get it, he called, "And bring me, please, a piece of bread."*
>
> *"As surely as the Lord your God lives," she replied, "I don't have any bread—only a handful of flour in a jar and a little olive oil in a jug. I am gathering a few sticks to take home and make a meal for myself and my son, that we may eat it—and die."*
>
> *Elijah said to her, "Don't be afraid. Go home and do as you have said. But first make a small loaf of bread for me from what you have and bring it to me, and then make something*

for yourself and your son. For this is what the Lord, the God of Israel, says: 'The jar of flour will not be used up and the jug of oil will not run dry until the day the Lord sends rain on the land.'"

She went away and did as Elijah had told her. So, there was food every day for Elijah and for the woman and her family. For the jar of flour was not used up and the jug of oil did not run dry, in keeping with the word of the Lord spoken by Elijah.

—1 Kings 17:7-16

Let me set the stage. There is a severe drought going on, and the brook where Elijah is staying is drying up. He must now move to a new location to find food and water. God speaks to him and directs him to "**Go at once to Zarephath in the region of Sidon and stay there. I have directed a widow there to supply you with food.**" It should be noted that Zarephath was a Canaanite town and was not part of the nation of Israel at the time.

As Elijah approaches the city, he sees a widow gathering sticks, and he calls out to her to give him some water. "***as she was going to get it, he called, 'And bring me, please, a piece of bread.'***" She answers that she is basically out of food, as there is only enough for one more meal for her son and herself.

But then the prophet does something extremely strange, something that you may even think is unthinkable considering the circumstances. He tells her to go home and make him a loaf and actually bring it to him before she makes one for her own family. Understanding how that may sound, he prefaces the instructions with the words, "*Don't be afraid.*" Then he declares to her the following:

> *For this is what the Lord, the God of Israel, says: "The jar of flour will not be used up and the jug of oil will not run dry until the day the Lord sends rain on the land."*

Wow, what will she do? Will she believe him and give him her son's last meal?

> *She went away and did as Elijah had told her. So, there was food every day for Elijah and for the woman and her family. For the jar of flour was not used up and the jug of oil did not run dry, in keeping with the word of the Lord spoken by Elijah.*

She did believe him, and pay close attention to the result—there was food every day for Elijah and for the woman and her family. Let me change one word and say that again, "There was food every day for God's assignment and food for the woman and her family."

We talked in the last chapter about the fear in giving, that there would not be enough for your needs if you gave into God's assignments. As you can see, and will always see, that is not going to happen!

So, let me ask you a question, "Did it cost the widow anything to give that last meal away?" No, it did not. It saved her life.

Now, before I get to our discussion concerning the word SENT, I want to ask another question. Why did the prophet insist that she make his cake *first*? Not *with* hers but *separate*. He even asked that she bring it to him *before* she started baking her own. (Remember, you want to be a spiritual scientist and ask questions.)

All these stories are showing you vital insights into Kingdom law and operation. Was Elijah just so hungry that he did not want to wait while she made a meal for the entire family? No, there was a very important reason why he did that. The prophet knew that when she gave him the first cake, before she made hers, that her action brought all of her flour and oil under the legal jurisdiction of the Kingdom of God and His assignment. Let me say that again.

When she gave the prophet (God's assignment) the first cake, her oil and flour changed kingdoms. They now came under the jurisdiction of the Kingdom of God. It was only then that God could legally make the flour and oil multiply.

You will see this same principle operate later in the ministry of Jesus when He feeds the 5,000 with the five loaves and two fish.

If you remember the story, Jesus told the disciples to go and see what they had. They came back and said they only had five loaves and two fish. Jesus told His disciples to bring the bread and fish to Him. The Bible records that He took them and blessed them and then gave them right back to the disciples. I know that Jesus did nothing religiously, so why did He do that?

He had to or the bread and fish could not have multiplied. You see, the five loaves and two fish were legally under the dominion of men at that time. God could not do anything legally with them. But when they were offered to Jesus freely and He blessed them, they came under the legal jurisdiction of the Kingdom of God. Then and only then could the bread and fish multiply.

The same principle can be seen in Luke chapter 5 where Peter, James, and John had fished all night and caught nothing. Borrowing Peter's boat, Jesus pushes a bit off the shore and preaches to the crowd, after which He tells Peter to cast his net over in the deep water for a catch of fish.

As you remember, they ended up with two boats so full of fish that they began to sink. When Jesus borrowed the boat, He was really borrowing the fishing business to preach from that day. The minute He took possession of it, the entire business came under the legal jurisdiction of the Kingdom of God. This made it legal for heaven to send a word of knowledge to Jesus as to where the fish were at, thus the huge catch. (I always say that anyone can catch fish if Jesus tells them where they are and how to catch them. This is the same principle you will be using as well when you give toward God's assignments.)

Now, going back to our story with Elijah, this widow essentially partnered with Elijah and his assignment and thus reaped the same reward he did. There was then provision for Elijah AND the widow and her family. Do you see it?

I will talk more about this principle a little later in this book, but I want to go on to the big key in this story, the word SENT.

Let's review. God had Elijah on assignment. He needed provision to carry out His assignment. We know that Elijah was a prophet, so he carried the word of the Lord wherever God would send him. But God needed His assignment funded, and that always involves *people*.

In this case, God could not find a widow in Israel who would have the faith to obey Him. God knew what He wanted to do, but He had to have someone come into agreement with heaven to make it legal for Him to bring the provision that Elijah needed.

Remember, there was no food anywhere. People were dying everywhere. It was not a matter of just finding some food, or going to the market, because there was not any food. Elijah's provision had to come by the Spirit of God.

Since there was no one in Israel who had the faith to believe Him, God had to go outside of Israel to another nation where He found a widow who had a heart of faith. And as we said earlier, Elijah was sent to this specific widow because God knew she would believe Him.

By putting God first and obeying the word of the Lord to her, God's assignment, Elijah, was taken care of as well as her family throughout the entire famine.

So here is the point of the story...

When God has things to get done, He looks over the earth to find someone that He can trust, someone that will obey Him and carry out His plans. He also needs people who will finance His agenda.

So, let me make this very clear: If you want to have big ideas, if you want God to download great business concepts to you, you have to qualify for them! God knows your heart, and He is looking over the earth for those He can trust with His assignments. He is looking to see who He can trust to fund His assignments. He will then send that person the plan He has for gathering the money that is needed. Do you see it?

Remember, the word of the Lord was SENT to this widow, and it saved her life!

I remember the word of the Lord coming to me to step out and start my business with a new priority and mandate. I did, and it saved my life.

God looks for those who have hearts of obedience to fund His assignments!

Let's review the principles we see in this story.

1. God has assignments in the earth realm He wants to accomplish.
2. Every assignment needs people.
3. Every assignment needs funding.
4. God is looking over the earth to find those people who will carry out His assignments.
5. And God is looking over the earth for those who will fund His assignments.
6. When we fund God's assignments, we are giving heaven legal jurisdiction not only to use us to fund God's assignment, but the overflow then also funds our own lives as well.

It will never cost you to be generous! I tell my church, "Always say yes."

CHAPTER 4
WHOSE MONEY IS IT?

Have you ever had the realization that some of the money you have right now is not yours?

I know that sounds crazy, but have you ever realized that God may have put that money in your hands for someone else?

I know, I know, you probably have not really thought about life from that perspective, but you should because it is another key to increase in your life.

Think about what I am saying. We have been talking about funding God's assignments, right? And we said that God is looking over the earth to find people who have hearts for the Kingdom and will fund His assignments. We know that money is in the hands of men, and if God is going to fund His assignments, He has to get money into the hands of people who are willing to let go of it and be generous toward Him and His people.

So, what is in your hands? When you look at what you have, do you realize that God may have put that there for someone else? Or that He may have brought it to you to fund a project He wants accomplished?

Of course, legally, what you have is yours and yours to decide what you want to do with it. But if God is going to put money in people's hands, I want to be on His approved list. Don't you?

> *Now he who supplies seed to the sower and bread for food will also supply and increase your store of seed and will enlarge the harvest of your righteousness.* You will be enriched in every way so that you can be generous on every occasion, and through us your generosity will result in thanksgiving to God.
>
> —2 Corinthians 9:10-11

We have already looked at this text, but there is something here that you may have missed. Verse 10 says that God *supplies* seed to the sower and bread for eating.

Think about what that is saying: God gives seed to the sower and bread for eating. The bread for eating represents all that you need in your own household to live the abundant life God has for you. But He gives *seed to the sower.*

Have you ever sown a garden or sown grass seed in your yard? You begin to put seed into the earth, and as you are sowing, you keep reaching for another handful of seed as you sow what you already have in your hand. There is a certain flow to it. As you let go of the seed in your hand, your hand is then filled with a fresh supply that you then sow also. This phrase, *God gives seed to the sower,* has the same connotation, meaning God is giving seed to someone who is in the process of sowing.

GOD GIVES SEED TO THE ONE THAT IS SOWING!

Paul goes on and says that God also gives us the bread we need, of course, but the emphasis in this passage is on sowing and the impact it has on our lives as well as on those we are generous toward. As we have already said, it moves people's hearts toward God.

With that in mind, I think we all can agree that God wants to sow as much seed as possible so that He can reap a huge harvest. So, if you were God, who would you give seed to? The one that is lazy and never gets around to sowing or the one that is actively sowing? I think the answer is obvious.

As we are faithful with what we have, God says that He will increase our store of seed so that we can sow more and have a bigger impact here in the earth for His Kingdom.

Did you notice that Paul says that as you are sowing and harvesting, your store of seed will increase, which will enable you to be generous on every occasion? If this is true (and it is, of course), then your store of seed is the money you are holding right now for that opportunity to be generous to show up. Your store of seed has to be in place before you can be generous.

Again, my point is that the money you are holding is not all yours. Some of it has been given to you by God to be seed. This cycle of sowing and reaping is a flow. We sow, then we reap; and as we continue to do so, as long as we do not eat our seed, our harvest will keep increasing, and so will our ability to be more generous.

Of course, when you are hungry and needing bread, you take from your seed business what you need as well. As your seed business increases, your ability to take bread from it also increases.

But I want to go a bit deeper into this mindset.

Let me make the point that God gives His seed to the one that has a heart to sow, not the one that might consider it someday. He gives it to the sower.

So here is the question: Do you want to live your life handling just *your* money, or do you want to live your life handling yours and God's money?

James and Ella came to our church because they were hearing things that they had never heard in the Amish community where they both grew up. The Kingdom concepts were all new to them, and they were great students of the Kingdom. They would listen over and over again to the messages we taught on Kingdom living at Faith Life Church.

DO YOU WANT TO LIVE YOUR LIFE ONLY HANDLING YOUR MONEY OR YOUR AND GOD'S MONEY?

One day, James told the Lord that he was hearing all these stories from others about how the Kingdom did great things in their lives, and he wanted to have that same testimony. He decided he was going to test the Kingdom laws he was hearing. They went on vacation and spent most of that time listening to the messages that pertained to the double portion, which I was teaching at that time. My book, *Your Financial Revolution: The Power of Rest* had just come out, and I was teaching from it. So they decided that they were just going to immerse themselves in the Word before they sowed a seed.

They decided that they were going to sow toward a harvest of $10,000, which they needed for some repairs and other needs that all families with young children have. They did not know where the money would come from, but they had been studying the Kingdom long enough by then that they felt they had faith for it.

At that time, James owned his own auto repair business. As he was leaving for work, not long after they had sown for that $10,000, he admitted to Ella that after studying the double portion, he really felt that they should believe for the double portion on their seed. He said he was believing for a $20,000 return. Ella said she was a little shocked, but she went along with her husband. As he was walking out the door, she said, "Okay, $20,000."

That day was just another day at the shop. One of James's regular customers came in with a repair, and as he finished writing up the order, his customer sat down in James's office and told him how frustrated he had been lately with his cows. Apparently, they had broken down all his fencing and had gotten out. His property bordered the national forest, so these cows were able to wander wherever they wanted. James's customer was an older gentleman, who then went on to say that he was just getting too old to keep chasing those cows around, and he was done with them. His next words shocked James to the point he had to ask himself if he heard his friend right.

His friend said, "I am done with these cows, and that is why I am giving them all to you today. From this day forth, they are yours." James did not know what to say. He had no land. He lived in town on a quarter-acre lot, and he was an auto mechanic. Yes, he grew up Amish and had grown up around cows, but that had been a number of years prior. He was about to say no thanks when he remembered their seed. Maybe there was something here that he needed to check out.

After questioning his friend further, he found out that there were 23 Black Angus cows and three horses in the deal. James remembered someone saying to him a while back that they were looking for a herd of cattle to buy. They did not want to buy a few at a time but were interested in taking over someone else's herd. James gave them a call and, yes, the man said he would be interested. James then asked him what he would be willing to give for the cattle, and the man thought for a moment and then said, "Oh, probably $20,000."

James could not believe what he was hearing. This all happened after he left home that day and told Ella of the double portion nudge from the Holy Spirit. He told me it was quite a chore to get the cows rounded up and then trucked to their new home, but he got it done. James then told me that he was absolutely convinced that the Kingdom of God could do anything and that he was no longer limited by his own potential.

When he went home that first day and told Ella about the cows, he said she was just shocked. If you would ask James and Ella about the grace of God, you had better have a few hours to spare because they would have a lot to say.

This is a great example of the Holy Spirit showing a person where to reap the harvest on their generosity toward God. Once we sow, we may need to remember that what the Holy Spirit shows us may just be, for lack of a better word, *crazy*! I mean, there was no way that James was going to come up with that idea with his pencil and paper working through his T-bar and mentally looking at the options.

Take Peter for instance. I am sure in his wildest thoughts he would have never thought about looking in a fish's mouth to find the coin to pay his taxes, or that a Rabbi walking down the seashore would be able to tell him exactly where to cast his net for the catch of a lifetime.

Look at Drenda and me being in debt during those nine years of stress and turmoil. The thought that we would someday own a company that helped people get out of debt or, even more shocking, have a television broadcast that was on in every time zone in the world titled, *Fixing the Money Thing*, would be impossible.

You never want to limit God.

So, let's review, and remember that God gives seed to the sower— the one who is sowing and desiring to sow!

Let's move on. I want to look now at what I personally consider to be one of the most profound parables that Jesus ever taught about God working with people and how they must qualify to be used. This one definitely makes you stop and think.

Jesus told his disciples: "There was a rich man whose manager was accused of wasting his possessions. So he called him in and asked him, 'What is this I hear about you? Give an account of your management, because you cannot be manager any longer.'

The manager said to himself, "What shall I do now? My master is taking away my job. I'm not strong enough to dig, and I'm ashamed to beg—I know what I'll do so that, when I lose my job here, people will welcome me into their houses."

So he called in each one of his master's debtors. He asked the first, "How much do you owe my master?"

"Nine hundred gallons of olive oil," he replied.

The manager told him, "Take your bill, sit down quickly, and make it four hundred and fifty."

Then he asked the second, "And how much do you owe?"

"A thousand bushels of wheat," he replied.

He told him, "Take your bill and make it eight hundred."

The master commended the dishonest manager because he had acted shrewdly. For the people of this world are more shrewd in dealing with their own kind than are the people of the light. I tell you, use worldly wealth to gain friends for yourselves, so that when it is gone, you will be welcomed into eternal dwellings.

Whoever can be trusted with very little can also be trusted with much, and whoever is dishonest with very little will also be dishonest with much. So if you have not been trustworthy in handling worldly wealth, who will trust you with true riches? And if you have not been trustworthy with someone else's property, who will give you property of your own?

No one can serve two masters. Either you will hate the one and love the other, or you will be devoted to the one and despise the other. You cannot serve both God and money.

The Pharisees, who loved money, heard all this and were sneering at Jesus. He said to them, "You are the ones who justify yourselves in the eyes of others, but God knows your hearts. What people value highly is detestable in God's sight."

—Luke 16:1-15

There is so much in this parable to look at. First, we see that a wealthy owner had put a manager in charge of his operations, and apparently, the manager was wasting the owner's possessions and had disqualified himself from managing any further. Knowing that he was losing his job, he quickly called all those who owed his boss money and told them they could settle the bill for a huge discount, sometimes half if they did it quickly.

Now, of course, the owner was totally unaware of what the manager was doing. But the dishonest manager thought if he gave these other people a great deal, they would look favorably on him once he left the owner, and he hoped they might offer him a job in their operation. When the owner heard what the dishonest manager had done, he called him in and:

The master commended the dishonest manager because he had acted shrewdly.

The definition of shrewd is: Having or showing a clever awareness or resourcefulness, especially in practical matters. Disposed to or marked by artful and cunning practices; tricky.[11]

The owner saw that the manager had the ability to create and

---

[11] *The American Heritage® Dictionary of the English Language, Fifth Edition*

carry out a plan that would produce a profit, in this case not for the owner but himself—something he had not seen from this manager on his behalf. However, when it came to taking care of himself, he was on it and was, in fact, very clever and detailed. He showed initiative concerning his own affairs and his own well-being but showed none of that on behalf of his master. Let me be blunt here—he was a hireling!

Now, let me ask the really hard question: Are you a Christian hireling?

Are you more concerned about your well-being than you are about God's business? Are you more concerned about your own cares and concerns than you are about God's cares and concerns? Are you wasting God's possessions?

Wow, I know those are tough questions. That is why I said this parable is so profound, because it cuts right to the heart and reveals any wrong attitudes that may be hidden there.

Jesus gives us the picture and defines what a hireling is in John 10:11-13.

> *I am the good shepherd. The good shepherd lays down his life for the sheep. The hired hand is not the shepherd and does not own the sheep. So when he sees the wolf coming, he abandons the sheep and runs away. Then the wolf attacks the flock and scatters it. The man runs away because he is a hired hand and cares nothing for the sheep.*
>
> —John 10:11-13

The NKJV (v. 13) says it this way:

> *The hireling flees because he is a hireling and does not care about the sheep.*

In the case of the dishonest manager, he was disqualified from handling the owner's money because he really did not care for the owner's well-being; he only cared for his own. Now, he still had the ability to go out and make his own money, of course, but he would no longer have the opportunity to handle his AND the owner's money.

I believe we are living in a time when the hireling mentality is running wild in America and in the world.

I am sure you have been in a restaurant and have seen dirty tables and a dirty floor, and in the back, you saw a few employees goofing off. Or you pull into a fast food restaurant maybe 30 minutes before closing, and you are shocked to see all the chairs on top of the tables and the employees lined up at the time clock waiting to leave. You know, without asking, the owner is not there. These are all hirelings. They do not care for the profit of the business. They are there to get a paycheck and that is all.

So many employers tell me it is getting so bad that if an employee just shows up for work on time, he will stand out in the crowd. Employers are crying out for owners, not takers. They want employees who will work and care like they are running their own businesses. They tell me that an employee who carries himself or herself with that kind of attitude would be promoted and sought out.

God is no different. He is looking for people who care for what He cares for and hates what He hates.

In 1 Samuel 15, God tells King Saul to attack the Amalekites for what they did to Israel on their way out of Egypt. King Saul was told not to leave the king and the men alive. They were not to bring any of the animals back with them, but that is what Saul did:

But Saul and the army spared Agag and the best of the sheep and cattle, the fat calves and lambs—everything that was good.

These they were unwilling to destroy completely, but everything that was despised and weak they totally destroyed.

—1 Samuel 15:9

Look at what God then says in verses 10-11:

Then the word of the Lord came to Samuel: "I regret that I have made Saul king, because he has turned away from me and has not carried out my instructions."

Then we see God speaking to Samuel about Saul in 1 Samuel 16:1.

The Lord said to Samuel, "How long will you mourn for Saul, since I have rejected him as king over Israel? Fill your horn with oil and be on your way; I am sending you to Jesse of Bethlehem. I have chosen one of his sons to be king."

Just as the dishonest manager was disqualified to handle the owner's affairs, so Saul was disqualified. And guess what? You and I can be disqualified as well.

What is God looking for? Who will He trust?

After removing Saul, he made David their king. God testified concerning him: "I have found David son of Jesse, a man after my own heart; he will do everything I want him to do."

—Acts 13:22

If we can be disqualified, we can also be qualified. You may say, "Well, Gary how do I do that?" This parable answers that question for you.

> *Whoever can be trusted with very little can also be trusted with much, and whoever is dishonest with very little will also be dishonest with much. So if you have not been trustworthy in handling worldly wealth, who will trust you with true riches? And if you have not been trustworthy with someone else's property, who will give you property of your own?*
>
> *No one can serve two masters. Either you will hate the one and love the other, or you will be devoted to the one and despise the other. You cannot serve both God and money.*
>
> —Luke 16:10-13

Let me be clear: You must pass the loyalty test. If you can be trusted with very little, you can be trusted with much. The test always begins with the natural and moves into the spiritual. You must be trustworthy in handling worldly wealth before God will trust you with His wealth. If you are not trustworthy with someone else's property, who will give you property of your own? Certainly not God.

Okay, here comes the application of the parable to our own lives.

Most Christians give God the leftovers.

Most Christians look at their budgets and decide, "This is what I can give." Yet they have no trouble going out the same day and buying a brand-new boat.

Now, I am not trying to make anyone feel condemned, and God certainly does not care if you have a nice boat. I am simply asking you: Do you want to just handle your money or yours and God's?

If you Google what the average Christian gives, you may be shocked. I saw one stat that said the average Christian gives just over

$13 a week to church.[12]

I looked at many stats regarding giving, and they were all disappointing. As I said, most Christians give God their leftovers. Again, please understand I am not trying to bring condemnation or evoke guilt. I am just making a point—and I think the Word of God upholds my viewpoint—that God is not looking for hirelings; He is looking for owners.

Secondly, God is not looking for people that feel compelled to give out of guilt. God loves a cheerful giver, according to 2 Corinthians 9:7.

Saul was disqualified for not doing what God asked, but David was chosen because he would obey and do what God needed done.

So, let me propose a new perspective. What if we turned our world upside down and decided to live for God first and that we would be the ones who live on the leftovers? I can only surmise that your leftovers would soon overtake you and you would live a blessed life.

It worked for R.G. LeTourneau. From humble beginnings and only a seventh grade education, he taught himself and, eventually, built a manufacturing empire. His earth-moving machines helped win WWII and construct the highway infrastructure of modern America. By the end of his life, he held 300 patents.[13]

His secret? He gave God 90% of all that he made.[14]

Now, I am not telling you to do the same. This was an agreement that he and God made when he was 30 years old and was deeply in

---

[12] https://www.pastorrickypowell.com/life_matters_with_pastor_/2009/10/startling-statistics

[13] http://centerforfaithandwork.com/article/who-was-rg-letourneau

[14] https://centerforfaithandwork.com/article/why-rg-letourneau-gave-90-percent

debt. He made God his business partner (as he calls it), and it paid off.

When God called me to start a church from scratch, I was already running my company, Forward Financial Group. It had become very successful and had become number one out of 5,000 offices nationwide with our primary vendor. When God called me to pastor, I asked him, "What about Forward Financial Group? Should I close it down and focus on pastoring my church?"

The Lord answered me and said, *"No, keep it going as it helps many people."* So I did.

I will admit that at times it was hard to do both, but it has helped thousands upon thousands of people over the years. As I pastored our church, I assumed that the company would decline in production with me having to drastically cut my involvement. But as Drenda and I laid our lives down to accomplish God's mandates, I found just the opposite. Even though I was working only in my spare time with the company, it was still performing at a stellar rate.

Out of hundreds of offices, we would be in the top five to ten offices nationwide and would be recognized on stage. Yet I had to smile, knowing that I did this part time and I pastored more than full time. God honored me with favor and wisdom so that those in the world who were pursuing money with all their hearts had to stop and wonder how I did it.

I can remember sitting at a table at one convention and the guy sitting next to me asking me how much marketing I did. I had to smile as I said, "None." He then asked, "Then how do you do so much business?" I told him we just worked word of mouth and that God blessed us. He just shook his head as he just could not figure me out.

One time, the president of one of our vendors called and wanted to know if I would address the convention attendees on how I was able to produce so much. I said I would be glad to. He then began to ask me questions about how our operation worked and how we did the business we did. Of course, I had to tell him how we trusted God and how He blessed us with favor. After I told him that I only worked a few hours a week and was a full-time pastor, he then said, "Well, I thought you must have a finely detailed marketing strategy laid out and you would be sharing how that worked. I do not think this is what I had in mind, but I appreciate your willingness to share." Oh well, that was their loss. I could have helped a lot of guys in there.

GOD SEES IT. IN EVERY ASSIGNMENT, YOU ARE TRAINING FOR THE NEXT, SO NEVER DESPISE THE DAY OF SMALL BEGINNINGS.

I have said throughout this book that if you take care of God's business, He will take care of yours!

So, let me ask you the question we started with, "Whose money is it?"

Would you rather just handle your own money, like the dishonest manager was left with, or do you want to handle God's money as well? When you handle God's money, your seed business gets energized by God's wisdom and grace, which allows your personal harvest of bread to also be pulled along with that increase.

I am convinced God does not care if you have millions as long as He has your heart!

Remember, it starts with the small assignments where no one knows your name. Even though you may think no one cares what you are doing in that part-time job, God sees it. In every assignment, you are training for the next, so never despise the day of small beginnings.

Approach it as if you owned it and give it your best. I guarantee you will shine like a star in the night and posture yourself for promotion and favor.

CHAPTER 5
YOU NEED A PARTNER!

As you know, I have been in the financial business for almost 40 years now. Through the years, I have had many people ask me how to start businesses and what makes a business grow.

Of course, there are many things people need to know, but the most important thing I could tell them is that they need a *partner*.

Now, as a pastor for many years, I have seen more than my share of people who thought it would be great to go into business with their church buddy, and then the whole thing imploded. Friends get offended by each other, and many times even stop talking, and the relationship is ruined. Because I have seen this so many times, I rarely suggest that you go into business with your friend unless you have the boundaries clearly laid out and written out.

However, there is a partner that I always insist you take on, and that is God.

In a previous chapter, we talked about the woman who received the prophet Elijah and gave him her last meal. We saw how that act of faith produced food every day for the prophet, God's assignment, and the woman's family. She partnered with him in his assignment, and in so doing, the anointing and provision that were on his assignment became hers. They were partners.

Throughout this book, we have been talking about being generous toward God and sowing into His assignments. I have also told you how being generous opens people's hearts toward you and toward God as well.

In this chapter, I want to share with you another powerful principle of the Kingdom of God that will propel your finances to a whole new level—the principle of partnership.

> One day as Jesus was standing by the Lake of Gennesaret, the people were crowding around him and listening to the word of God. He saw at the water's edge two boats, left there by the fishermen, who were washing their nets. He got into one of the boats, the one belonging to Simon, and asked him to put out a little from shore. Then he sat down and taught the people from the boat.
>
> When he had finished speaking, he said to Simon, "Put out into deep water, and let down the nets for a catch."
>
> Simon answered, "Master, we've worked hard all night and haven't caught anything. But because you say so, I will let down the nets."
>
> When they had done so, they caught such a large number of fish that their nets began to break. So they signaled their partners in the other boat to come and help them, and they came and filled both boats so full that they began to sink.
>
> —Luke 5:1-7

I know I already mentioned this story earlier when I talked about the boats and the fishing business changing kingdoms (or jurisdictions) when Peter (Simon) lent his boat to Jesus to preach from. I also mentioned the incredible catch of fish that occurred and almost sank the two boats. Remember, Peter said he had fished all night and caught nothing. Now, just a few hours later, he had so many fish that he couldn't pull them in fast enough. What was the difference? The Kingdom, of course, but also *partnership*. Let me explain.

> *He saw at the water's edge two boats, left there by the fishermen, who were washing their nets. He got into one of the boats, the one belonging to Simon, and asked him to put out a little from shore.*

Let's get the setting clear in our minds. Where were they, and what were they doing when Jesus came by? They were not fishing; they were on the shore washing their nets after fishing all night and catching nothing.

Jesus, noticing that the boats were available, asks Peter if he could put out from shore a bit so that He could preach from the boat to the crowd. So where were James and John, his partners, while he took Jesus out in the boat? Well, they were still on the shore with the other boat and their nets.

After preaching, Jesus told Peter to let down his nets for a catch over in the deep water. And you know the story. He began to catch so many fish that his nets almost broke. So he called his partners out to help him drag in the fish. And the Bible says that both boats almost sank, they were so full of fish.

> *When they had done so, they caught such a large number of fish that their nets began to break. So they signaled their partners in the other boat to come and help them, and they came and filled both boats so full that they began to sink.*

Now, here is the million-dollar question: How much faith did James and John exercise to cause their boat to be so filled that it almost sank?

Think about it—they were still on the shore with their nets. It was Peter who agreed to take Jesus out. He is the one who said, "*But because you say so, I will let down the nets.*" So the correct answer is none! James and John did not harvest that boatload of fish because of *their* faith; it was because of Peter's faith. Peter simply called to his partners who were on the shore to come and help bring in the fish. Amazingly, their boat filled <u>exactly</u> as Peter's had, to overflowing.

> *Simon answered, "Master, we've worked hard all night and haven't caught anything. But <u>because you say so</u>, I will let down the nets."*

So if it was Peter's faith that brought the fish and filled his boat, then why did James and John's boat fill up with the identical amount of fish as Peter's boat did?

The text answers that question—it says they were *partners*.

The definition of partner in the Collins English Dictionary is:

A person who shares or is associated with another in some action or endeavor; usually sharing its risks and profits.

A partnership is a legal entity and shares in the risks, costs, and profit of the business. So, when Peter gave Jesus the boat to use, he was really loaning Jesus the *business* in a legal sense, not just the boat. Technically, James and John also owned a part of the boat that Peter let Jesus use, and because of their partnership, both boats filled equally.

James and John reaped <u>exactly the same harvest</u> as Peter did even though they did not exercise faith in that situation at all. I bet they were glad that Peter was their partner that day. What do you think? I think so. Let me give you a more personal example of this principle.

Drenda and I own 60 beautiful acres with a mix of woods, marsh, and grassland. It is an absolutely perfect place to hunt deer. There are crops planted all around our property, and the woods and marsh are natural magnets for the deer.

I built my office over our garage, and it has wooden bookshelves and a built-in gas fireplace. It is a quiet, cozy, man cave type of office, which I love to work from. The only thing that was missing was a nice mounted buck over my desk. To be honest, I was never interested in shooting big bucks, as I was a meat hunter. And I had never shot a buck that really was big enough to warrant mounting.

We had lived on the property for five years when Drenda insisted that I shoot a big buck for my office. Up until that point, I had never seen a big buck on the property. I had been out every deer season and had shot a couple of nice eight-point bucks, but nothing that I would consider mounting class.

But that year, the more I thought about it, I agreed with Drenda. I told Drenda that I thought I would go for the big buck for the wall. Again, I had never seen a big buck in the woods. Our kitchen window faces the woods and the field, and yet I had never seen one.

So Drenda and I sowed for the big buck. I wrote on my seed check that I was sowing for a ten-point or bigger. We prayed over that seed, and I laid it on my desk to mail. That envelope sat there for three days, and I just couldn't mail it. I knew that I did not have faith for that ten-point. I had faith for an eight-, six-, or four-point all day long, but I was having trouble seeing that big buck with that assurance of faith that says, "I know that I know that I will shoot a ten-point or bigger buck when I go out."

I had enough experience with the Kingdom to know that I was not in faith. So, I tore that check up and replaced it with a check that said "for a four-point or bigger" and mailed it off.

The night before I was going out, I told Drenda what I had done. "I just do not have faith for that big buck," I told her. She looked at me and said, "*You* have faith for the deer, and *I* will have faith for the trophy buck. God is able to do immeasurably more than all you ask or think!"

The morning opened with the usual rustling of squirrels and birds in the woods as the smell of fall leaves took me back to many deer hunts in my mind. I hadn't sat there very long, maybe 20 minutes, when I heard the sound of a buck coming through the woods. The buck was heading straight for my tree, and I readied myself for the shot.

As the buck got closer, I saw that the buck was a four-point, exactly what I usually go for, as they are very good eating. The buck stepped into an opening at about 25 yards, and I let the arrow go. With disgust, I saw the arrow hit high and back, and I knew that I would have to track this one.

The buck took off through the woods and then jumped into the cornfield that bordered the woods and was out of sight. I could still hear it running through the corn and knew from how strong it was running that I might have a long tracking job ahead of me. I waited in the tree stand for about 20 minutes and then decided to get down out of the tree to inspect the arrow. I could tell I definitely hit the buck, and I spotted a trail of blood.

As I followed the blood trail, I was encouraged, as there was a good trail of blood. But after about 100 yards, the blood trail dried up. I looked and looked but could not find another drop. After two hours of looking, I realized that the buck was gone. I was so disappointed. First, I do not ever want to wound a deer and lose it, and secondly, I was disappointed with my shot.

As I stood there in the cornfield, I started to walk back toward the house when I had a thought. *I still have a chance, I may jump a deer as I make my way home through the cornfield and then the marsh area.*

I loaded my crossbow just in case. And as I slowly made my way along the weeded gully, suddenly, a deer jumped up and dashed out in front of me. Not knowing what I was, the deer stopped and looked back. Since I had camouflage on, the deer, which I could see was a buck, hesitated as it could not make me out. It all happened in a split second, but I could see antlers, although I could not tell how big they were or how many points there were.

I knew that I had but a split second to make my mind up about the buck. He was beyond my normal bow range at about 55 yards and standing broadside to me. I quickly pulled up and aimed at the top of his back and let the arrow go.

The buck dropped instantly as the arrow hit and stayed down. I was kind of in shock. Did that really just happen?

As I walked up to the buck, the first thing I said was, "Drenda's faith!" The buck was huge! I counted 26 points, and he had drop tines as well. I had never seen a buck as big as this one! To say I was thrilled would not give the moment justice.

As you can guess, the buck is now over my desk in my office.

But I want to talk about this deer for a minute. How or why did he show up?

The four-point showed up right on time even though I messed up the shot. But Drenda said she was believing for the trophy buck.

Now, she had an advantage over me. She does not hunt deer, so to her, a trophy buck should be as easy as a four-point since they are all just deer to her. Because she does not hunt, she did not have an arguing picture of impossibility talking back to her. I had never seen even a big eight-point on the property, but her faith was not based on what was on the property or not. She believed that God could bring it.

This hunt took place during deer breeding season, the rut as it is called, and bucks can travel for miles looking for does. So there is always a good chance that in the rut, you will see bucks that you normally do not see on your property, as was the case here.

Drenda's faith brought that buck in even though I had no faith for that trophy buck.

I want you to read that again—I had no faith for that trophy buck!

I know what you are thinking—*Hold on, Gary. I am confused. If you had no faith for that buck, then why did it show up?*

The same way that James and John's boat filled by Peter's faith.

That is the power of partnership.

Let me give you one more example, and then we can talk about it.

> *I thank my God every time I remember you. In all my prayers for all of you, I always pray with joy because of your part-nership in the gospel from the first day until now, being confident of this, that he who began a good work in you will carry it on to completion until the day of Christ Jesus.*
>
> *It is right for me to feel this way about all of you, since I have you in my heart and, whether I am in chains or defending and confirming the gospel, all of you share in God's grace with me.*
>
> —Philippians 1:3-7

Paul says he remembers the church at Philippi with joy because of their continuing partnership with his ministry. He goes on to state that, because of their partnership, they now shared in God's grace that was on his ministry.

Remember we said that grace is God's empowerment or God's ability that was on Paul to accomplish his assignment? The church at Philippi was sharing the expense of the assignment and, like James and John, they also shared in the anointing and grace that was on that assignment.

Now let's go over to chapter four, and you will see the amazing result that partnership produces.

> *Yet it was good of you to share in my troubles. Moreover, as you Philippians know, in the early days of your acquaintance with the gospel, when I set out from Macedonia, not one church shared with me in the matter of giving and receiving, except you only; for even when I was in Thessalonica, you sent me aid more than once when I was in need. Not that I desire your gifts; what I desire is that more be credited to your account. I have received full payment and have more than enough. I am amply supplied, now that I have received from Epaphroditus the gifts you sent. They are a fragrant offering, an acceptable sacrifice, pleasing to God. <u>And my God will meet all your needs according to the riches of his glory in Christ Jesus</u>.*
>
> —Philippians 4:14-19

Paul had just received another contribution from the Philippian church. Listen to what he says back to them. "*My* God will meet all your needs."

Notice that Paul did not say, "*Your* God will meet your needs because you have been generous to me." NO! He said, "Now, *My* God will meet your needs!"

You see, the Philippians were partners with Paul, and as partners, they shared in that grace on Paul's assignment. Now, like James and John catching all those fish because of Peter's faith, Paul is declaring that their needs will be met because of *his* faith!

I hope you can see the advantage of this principle.

Let's assume you need a car, and you partner with us as a ministry. Let's also assume the car costs $30,000. Now, when you sow into GaryKeesee.com, you have an understanding of what partnership means—you share in the anointing and grace on our ministry.

As a ministry, we can easily agree on that $30,000, because we passed needing $30,000 a long time ago. We easily have faith for $30,000 as we spend millions annually now. But back in the day, I can remember having to believe God for $30,000, which at the time seemed like a huge mountain.

So, if you asked me if I could believe God for $30,000, the answer would be absolutely. So like Paul, when we are in agreement and we are partners, I can declare that your need is met, not because of *your* faith but because of *mine*.

Now obviously, you need to be in faith when you sow the seed toward that $30,000, and you have to have confidence not only in the Word of God but in us as well. You should have faith in me, confident that I am anointed and called of God, that I operate in integrity, and you should be able to see *demonstrated results* in my life and in my ministry. If you looked at what we are doing and where we came from, you know I have faith for $30,000!

You may not have $30,000 faith, but we can work together in partnership and see things that are amazing. It was the same for the trophy buck. Drenda said the night before I went out, "You believe for the deer, and I will believe for the trophy buck." This is how partnership works.

So let me lay some ground rules here by asking you a question: If you were going to start a computer company, would you want a guy who has no money and is in his first semester of computer science classes to be your partner or someone who has built a multimillion-dollar computer business and has the finances to help with your company launch?

Of course there are many variables here, and I am only making an illustration. But I think, on the surface, the obvious choice would be someone that has experience, has a proven track record, and was not going broke! The same is true when you want to sow into a ministry partnership.

Please do not confuse what I am saying in regard to a direct leading of God to partner with someone. That kind of leading supersedes what I am talking about. Many times, God will lead you to partner with His assignments, but sometimes you get to pick. I am talking specifically about sowing as a *choice* you make, sowing when you need a harvest and desire to move to the next level.

I sow into assignments that I believe in for the express purpose of accelerating the funds needed in my own life. One rule I do not break is I always sow into an assignment that understands faith and agreement when I want to accelerate my harvest. This kind of giving is *targeted* giving and is not to be confused with giving to the poor.

Giving to the needy is God's heart, and there is a return on that, but I am looking for a partnership with an assignment that has evidence of faith, that I know has the capacity to agree with me.

Think of it this way: If I asked someone who was making $3 an hour and was broke and had been broke for years to agree with me for $10 million, what would be the chance of actual agreement taking place?

Now, I can minister to anyone, and I am called to do that, but when it comes to agreement, there has to be agreement. A farmer does not sow his seed into just any field of dirt. He is looking for the right soil that his intended harvest requires. I am talking about partnering here in the earth realm with someone else's faith, someone else's anointing.

Another thing I will look for when I sow is a God assignment that has the same fruit that I am believing God for myself.

For instance, my company owns two airplanes. Before I bought either one of them, I sowed into a God assignment, a ministry that I knew had paid for dozens of multimillion-dollar planes in the past. When I say many, I mean *many*; and they were all paid for with cash. They had a demonstrated result when it came to planes. I knew they could easily agree with me for a plane and be in faith for it to come to pass. I wasn't going to partner with a ministry that said planes were too expensive, or not worth owning, or owning an airplane is of the devil. That is not any kind of agreement. No, I wanted to be in agreement with a ministry that understood where I was, could relate to me believing God for a plane, and had the fruit to prove it.

I have been a pilot since I was 19 years old and learned to fly off of a 3,000 foot gravel runway out in the country. I rented planes all my life until one day I thought, *Hey, you know what? I just need to sow a seed and believe God for my own plane.*

That is just what I did. I knew the exact plane I was going to sow for, so I wrote that exact plane on my check, and Drenda and I agreed on it. We then sent that check to the ministry that I just mentioned.

About a month went by, and I had a routine doctor's visit. As I was talking to the doctor that day, he casually said, "Do you happen to know anyone who would like to buy an airplane?"

I was a little surprised by the question, as I have never in all my life had someone ask me if I knew anyone who wanted to buy an airplane. I asked what kind of plane it was, and it was the exact plane I had sown my seed for.

Obviously, this had my attention. I went and looked at the plane, contacted the owner, and he took me on a flight. It was perfect. There was only one problem—at the time, I did not have the money to pay for it.

But God had a plan. In the previous fall, (it was now March), I had obtained a house from my father that I was going to rehab into an office building in the spring. My dad told me that he had turned off the water before winter, so I never checked it.

Just a few days after I looked at the plane, my brother called and said my house was ruined. He went on to tell me that all of the drywall in the house had been ruined, and most of it had fallen off the walls.

Apparently, the water was not turned off and the pipes had frozen in the winter. Now that it was March and warming up, the water had been running in the house for who knows how long, at least a few weeks.

What my brother did not know was that I had already signed a contract with a building company to strip the entire house of its drywall and the outside siding as part of the rebuilding process to convert the house into my new office complex.

Now, here is where the cool thing happened: The insurance company paid a claim for the water damage, and that was the cash that I used to pay for my airplane.

The plane was purchased with cash!

So remember, partnership is a powerful spiritual principle you will want to be aware of and take advantage of.

CHAPTER 6
THE MYSTERY OF THE TITHE

I receive emails frequently from people trying to convince me that this law of the Kingdom—the tithe—has passed away and is no longer valid.

However, I have found this Kingdom principle so important that I have dedicated an entire chapter to it.

I know that you, if you have been around church life at all, have heard of the tithe. But I also know that what you have heard is probably not completely accurate, and it is important that we straighten out some of the old religious mindsets about the tithe before we continue.

First of all, if you do not know, the word tithe actually means a tenth. The word was used to describe to God's people the amount of their income they were to give to His work, a tenth, or a tithe.

Now, this explanation of the tithe is in very simple terms, and I want to dig much deeper into this topic in this chapter. But for now, if this concept is new to you, this is basically what the tithe is, giving a tenth to God.

Secondly, when most people think of the tithe, they also think of the Old Testament and the Law of Moses where the tithe was required in the nation of Israel for all citizens.

Today, there is much confusion in the body of Christ around the tithe, what it is, and whether it is still in effect or passed away with the coming of Jesus.

As you've probably heard me say, when God told me to learn all I could about how His Kingdom operated, I really became a spiritual scientist. I wanted to know how everything worked, and the tithe was a big question that I had to answer.

So let's take a look at the tithe, where it came from, what it does, and why it is for today.

Although we actually see the tithe very prominently in the Law of Moses as a written requirement, the tithe did not begin with the Law of Moses. To find its origin, we need to go back to the beginning and the lives of Adam and Eve.

As mentioned previously, <u>Adam was created and set in the earth as the ruler over the earth on behalf of the Kingdom of God.</u>

> *You made them a little lower than the angels; you crowned them with glory and honor and put everything under their feet. In putting everything under them, God left nothing that is not subject to them.*
>
> —Hebrews 2:7-8a

Adam was crowned with glory and honor, and there was nothing on the earth that was not subject to him. The term *crowned* gives us a great picture of how this functioned.

If you look at a natural king, he wears a crown, and, although he's just a man, the crown indicates that the entire government backs up his words. So it was with Adam. He ruled the earth with complete authority, with heaven backing up all that he did. We must remember that in himself, he was just a man and ruled only through delegated authority. He had the glory (power) and the honor (position and authority) of the Kingdom of God backing him up.

Interestingly, we see Satan already on the earth when Adam was created, as he had been cast down to the earth before the creation of man. Satan despised this lowly creature (in the natural) that ruled over him on behalf of the Kingdom of God. He wanted to find a way to take that authority from Adam, basically to nullify Adam's authority to rule.

Of course, Satan had no power to undermine or overthrow Adam's position, so he had to devise a plan to deceive Eve into believing that God could not be trusted and that she and Adam should rebel against God and follow him.

Satan's plan was successful. Adam and Eve rebelled against God and lost their placees of authority. At that moment, since the entire earth realm was under Adam's dominion, Adam basically kicked God out of the earth as far as God's spiritual authority was concerned, and man was separated from God.

Much happened spiritually at that moment, but I do not have time to cover it here as I want to focus on our topic of the tithe. So let's go back to that moment when Adam and Eve fell and find out what happened.

> *To Adam he said, "Because you listened to your wife and ate fruit from the tree about which I commanded you, 'You must not eat from it,' cursed is the ground because of you; through painful toil you will eat food from it all the days of your life. It will produce thorns and thistles for you, and you will eat the plants of the field. By the sweat of your brow you will eat your food until you return to the ground, since from it you were taken; for dust you are and to dust you will return."*
>
> —Genesis 3:17-19

In a quick glance, we see that man lost his provision (was kicked out of the garden), his purpose then became survival, and he was then to survive by his own painful toil and sweat. God also told him that he would return to the ground, that he would *die* someday. The concepts of death and painful survival were totally foreign to Adam, and fear and hopelessness entered the world.

As you can see, and as Adam found out, the world had drastically changed.

I now want to go to Luke 4 where we will find another very important change that took place.

> *The devil led him up to a high place and showed him in an instant all the kingdoms of the world. And he said to him, "I will give you all their authority and splendor; it has been given to me, and I can give it to anyone I want to. If you worship me, it will all be yours."*
>
> —Luke 4:5-7

In this passage, Satan claims that all the money pertaining to the kingdoms of the earth (nations) are under his jurisdiction and states that this authority was given to him. And in that statement he is correct, as it was Adam who gave this authority to him in his rebellion.

Notice this verse says that all the splendor of the nations or kingdoms of the world were now under his jurisdiction. What is the splendor of a nation? Its *wealth*.

All the money in the earth realm has a kingdom, a nation, stamped on it, so all money is part of or under the jurisdiction of an earthly kingdom. Satan now claims that the money, or the wealth, of the nations are under his jurisdiction, and he claims he can give it to whomever he wants. To put it simply, Satan claims jurisdiction over the wealth and prosperity of the nations. This is very important as we will find out that the tithe has a very specific purpose tied to that fact.

> *Adam made love to his wife Eve, and she became pregnant and gave birth to Cain, She said, "With the help of the Lord I have brought forth a man." Later she gave birth to his brother Abel.*
>
> *Now Abel kept flocks, and Cain worked the soil. In the course of time Cain brought <u>some</u> of the fruits of the soil as an offering to the Lord. And Abel also brought an offering—<u>fat portions from some of the firstborn of his flock</u>. The Lord looked with favor on Abel and his offering, but on Cain and his offering he did not look with favor. So Cain was very angry, and his face was downcast.*
>
> *Then the Lord said to Cain, "Why are you angry? Why is your face downcast? <u>If you do what is right</u>, will you not be accepted? But if you do not do what is right, sin is crouching at your door; it desires to have you, but you must rule over it."*
>
> —Genesis 4:1-7

Okay, what was going on there? This was the first generation of kids. Why were they giving an offering? There was no written law stating to do so at that time, so why were they doing it?

We can assume that Adam and Eve, their parents, *taught* them to give offerings. We also can assume that God does not do things just for the ritual of doing them and there had to be a *legal* reason why Adam and Eve were taught to give offerings.

If you look at the text, you will see that there was a big difference in what the two boys brought to offer. Now, do not get hung up with what they had to offer, one offering animals and the other one offering plants, because that was not the issue. The issue was *how* they were offering what they had and why they were doing it in the first place.

Notice that Cain gave "some" of the fruit of the soil. But Abel brought the "fat portions from some of the firstborn" of his flock. Do you see the difference? In one case, it was "some" compared to the "best portion," which was the fat portion from the firstborn of the flock.

Why would Abel bring the fat portion, and why from the firstborn?

God must have told Adam the requirements for this offering.

Do you see it? This was the first time the tithe was seen.

If you study the tithe in the Law of Moses, it was always the **first** 10% given from **the best**. In this story, we can clearly see that Abel was giving the tithe, the *first* and the *best*. However, Cain was not happy to be giving up *some* of his crop and to have to honor God, and decided to bring "some" of his crops, not the first or the best.

Apparently, Cain knew what and how to offer the tithe to the Lord as God said to him, *"If you do what is right, will you not be accepted? But if you do not do what is right, sin is crouching at your door; it desires to have you, but you must rule over it."*

But Cain rejected God's encouragement to do what he had been taught and instead killed Abel, his brother. Possibly, he may have thought that with Abel out of the way, he could control both the field and the livestock, or his greed tempted him to bring only some of the crop, going through the motions of obedience with his heart far from God. I am only guessing. One thing we do know is that Cain did not want to tithe as he was taught.

At this point, you may be asking, "Why the tithe in the first place? Why did God require them to tithe?" I will answer those questions, but first, let's see what else we can learn about the tithe before we jump into those questions.

The next time we see the tithe show up is the first time the word *tithe* is actually used.

> *After Abram returned from defeating Kedorlaomer and the kings allied with him, the king of Sodom came out to meet him in the Valley of Shaveh (that is, the King's Valley). Then Melchizedek king of Salem brought out bread and wine. He was priest of God Most High, and he blessed Abram, saying, "Blessed be Abram by God Most High, Creator of heaven and earth. And praise be to God Most High, who delivered your enemies into your hand." Then Abram gave him a tenth of everything.*
>
> —Genesis 14:17-20

The question we need to ask here is: How did Abraham know to tithe and why?

Obviously, the tithe was passed down through the generations from Adam's time. And we know that the tithe was taught to Adam by God, Himself after the rebellion. Here we see the actual word tithe used, indicating a tenth was given.

Many people will say that the tithe was part of the Law of Moses, meaning that the New Testament believer is not under the need to tithe. The two incidents I have mentioned, Cain and Abel and then Abraham, prove that the tithe was given *before* the Law of Moses was written. Oh, I agree, the tithe was written into the Law of Moses, and the nation of Israel was required to tithe. But the tithe was something that the nation was already doing when Moses came on the scene.

So why was the tithe written into the Law of Moses? When the Law of Moses was written, it was to govern the entire life of the new nation of Israel that had just come out of Egypt. All of the legal and governing requirements were being set in its written code of conduct by which the people would live. Thus, the tithe was written into the Law of Moses to ensure it was being done as part of the life of the nation. The tithe was so important that God had it written into the law of the nation. We will find out why God wanted to make sure it was being done in a minute, but let's look at a few more examples of the tithe.

Now this is what the Lord Almighty says: "Give careful thought to your ways. You have planted much, but harvested little. You eat, but never have enough. You drink, but never have your fill. You put on clothes, but are not warm. You earn wages, only to put them in a purse with holes in it."

This is what the Lord Almighty says: "Give careful thought to your ways. Go up into the mountains and bring down timber and build my house, so that I may take pleasure in it and be honored," says the Lord. "You expected much, but see, it turned out to be little. What you brought home, I blew away. Why?" declares the Lord Almighty. "Because of my house, which remains a ruin, while each of you is busy with your own house. Therefore, because of you the heavens have withheld their dew and the earth its crops. I called for a drought on the fields and the mountains, on the grain, the new wine, the olive oil and everything else the ground produces, on people and livestock, and on all the labor of your hands."

—Haggai 1:5-11

In this passage, the prophet Haggai is rebuking the nation of Israel for not rebuilding the temple once they returned from exile in Babylon. They are not prospering, they are in lack, the crops are not good, and the whole nation is suffering. God tells the nation to give careful thought to **their ways**, implying that there was something they were doing or not doing that was causing the lack.

God says, "**_Because of you_** _the heavens have withheld their dew._" He says He had to call for the drought because of what **they** were doing. They were all building their own homes and yet leaving God's temple in ruins. This indicates that they were not tithing.

See, the tithe was to be brought to the Levites—the priests—and used for the temple ministry. Since the tithe was not being brought to the Levites, and the temple was not being built, God had to withdraw His hand of blessing because of what they were doing.

Make sure that you understand it was not God's will that He withdraw His blessing from the nation of Israel. He had no choice, as it was a legal issue involving the tithe.

As we continue to read in chapter two, we see that, apparently, the people began to heed the prophet's words.

> "_Now give careful thought to this from this day on—consider how things were before one stone was laid on another in the Lord's temple. When anyone came to a heap of twenty measures, there were only ten. When anyone went to a wine vat to draw fifty measures, there were only twenty. I struck all the work of your hands with blight, mildew and hail, yet you did not return to me," declares the Lord. "From this day on, from this twenty-fourth day of the ninth month, give careful thought to the day when the foundation of the Lord's temple was laid. Give careful thought: Is there yet any seed left in the barn? Until now,_

the vine and the fig tree, the pomegranate and the olive tree have not borne fruit. From this day on I will bless you."

—Haggai 2:15-19

Since they put the temple first again, God told them to mark the day and the hour because they were going to see a dramatic increase in their prosperity. He wanted them to mark the spot to encourage and motivate them to remember the change so they would not stop tithing again, not for His benefit but for their own.

There are some real keys here that will make sense in a minute, but the first thing I want you to realize is that the tithe is a *legal* issue. God *had* to withdraw His hand when they weren't tithing, not because He *wanted* to but because He *had* to.

"For I am the Lord, I do not change; therefore you are not consumed, O sons of Jacob. Yet from the days of your fathers you have gone away from My ordinances and have not kept them. Return to Me, and I will return to you," says the Lord of hosts.

"But you said, 'In what way shall we return?'

"Will a man rob God? Yet you have robbed Me!

But you say, 'In what way have we robbed You?'

In tithes and offerings. You are cursed with a curse, for you have robbed Me, even this whole nation. Bring all the tithes into the storehouse, that there may be food in My house, and try Me now in this," says the Lord of hosts, "If I will not open for you the windows of heaven and pour out for you such blessing that there will not be room enough to receive it. And I will rebuke the devourer for your sakes, so that he will not destroy the fruit of your ground, nor shall the vine fail to bear fruit for you in the field," says the Lord of hosts; "and all nations will call you

blessed, for you will be a delightful land," says the Lord of hosts.
—Malachi 3:6-12 (NKJV)

Here we see a different prophet rebuking the nation, stating that they are robbing God of His ability to bless His people. He says they—the whole nation—are under a curse because of what they are *not* doing. They are instructed to bring the whole tithe into the storehouse, that there may be food in God's house.

Again, the tithe was to be brought to the Levites, the priests. The people were bringing some but not the whole tithe (remember Cain's sin). The Lord is telling the people that if they will bring the whole tithe that the blessing of heaven will be theirs again. Heaven will have legal jurisdiction to move in their midst. God tells them that if they will return to Him with the tithe, then they will have such blessing they will not be able to contain it.

Okay, let's stop here and talk about this for a minute before I go any further.

So far, we have seen that the tithe was started clear back in the beginning, and now we can see why. Here we see the tithe gives God legal jurisdiction to step in between the devourer, Satan, and God's people and to rebuke Satan.

Basically, God was saying, "Hands off, Satan! You cannot touch their stuff!"

See, when Adam fell, Satan would have just loved to completely starve him off the planet. But, immediately, God put the tithe in place to protect Adam and Eve. When Adam and Eve chose to tithe, they were putting God first. They were choosing God.

Let's remember that Satan gained his entrance into the earth realm in the same manner. By convincing Adam and Eve to believe him instead of God, he gained legal entrance. So by tithing—giving

THE TITHE WAS PUT IN PLACE TO ACT AS A LEGAL FENCE AROUND ADAM AND EVE THEN, AND IT STILL ACTS AS A LEGAL SHIELD AROUND US TODAY.

God 10% of what they had—it gave God the legal right to protect Adam and Eve's provision.

We need to remember that the tithe was a law that pertained only to man's provision on the earth in Satan's territory. It did not change their status in regard to bringing spiritual restoration. No, a sacrifice for sin would have to be made first before that could happen. But the tithe did allow God to stop Satan from stealing provision from them, and it would allow them to survive on the earth.

Many people say that the tithe was an Old Testament law and has now passed away, being fulfilled by Jesus's sacrifice. But we have seen that the law of the tithe was put in place clear back at the fall of man before the Law of Moses was written.

The tithe was put in place to act as a legal fence around Adam and Eve then, and it still acts as a legal shield around us today.

The tithe is a law of the earth realm and remains in force as long as Satan is loose on the earth, as he currently is. As long as Satan is here, the law of the tithe is still in effect.

Another thing you may see in church are people who are tithing and yet not prospering. This is because of some wrong teaching in regard to the tithe. People think if they just tithe, the blessing of the Lord will cause them to enjoy overflowing prosperity, more than they could contain. When they begin to tithe and not see their prosperity overflowing, they conclude that the tithe does not work. But their assumption is not accurate, and we need to take a closer look at the text to find out why.

God told the people that if they tithed, "*I will prevent pests from devouring __your crops__, and the __vines in your fields__ will not drop their fruit before it is ripe."*

Do you see it? It says that the windows of heaven will be opened and God will bless *their* crops. The point I am making is that *you* still have to grow something inside the fence of the tithe.

The tithe by itself does not cause you to prosper. It only protects what you do inside of the fence, the tithe.

So if you have three tomato plants, they are going to prosper. But if all you have are three tomato plants, you will have three great plants, but you will not be prospering very much.

It is what *you* build or grow inside the fence that causes you to overflow with abundance.

Sadly, with wrong teaching, many of God's people tithe and then sit down with an iced tea and wait for the abundant overflow to begin. The overflow will begin when we understand our part in the process.

So again, let's review.

1. The tithe came into the earth at the beginning, at the fall of man.
2. It was written into the Law of Moses because the Law of Moses dictated how the nation of Israel lived. God, wanting to be sure He could bless them, wrote it into that law to ensure it continued. The law of the tithe has not passed away. But the legal requirement to tithe has. Now, we have the *choice* to tithe and take advantage of its benefit.
3. The law of the tithe is a law of the earth realm and will remain as long as Satan is on the loose.
4. The tithe does not automatically cause you to prosper,

but it does allow God to stop Satan from interfering with what you are growing or building inside the fence of the tithe.

5. The tithe has no bearing on if you go to heaven or not. You will go to heaven if you call on the name of Jesus. But the tithe will affect your prosperity here on the earth.

6. The tithe belongs to God's storehouse. In the Old Testament, it fed and took care of the priests who worked in the ministry. It is no different today. The tithe should be given to your home church. God has ordained the tithe to take care of the ministry.

   I have people tell me they don't like their church and ask if they have to tithe there. My answer? Find a new church, one that teaches faith and the Kingdom.

   If you are in between churches, you can tithe to a ministry that you are feeding from, but being in a good home church is God's best. If there are none in your area, then you can tithe, again, to where you are being fed.

7. You cannot name your tithe. For instance, as you sow your tithe, you can't say, "I am planting my tithe as a seed for _____." The tithe already has its assignment. You can name an offering but not the tithe.

8. The tithe is 10% of what you make. This is *before* taxes. Remember, God said through Malachi, "Bring *all* the tithe into the storehouse." Nine percent is not the tithe. Six percent is not the tithe. The tithe is 10%. If you say, "I cannot afford to pay that 10%," do what God was telling Israel to do when they were not bringing the whole tithe: "Test me in this," He said. Give your tithe by faith, knowing that God will honor it.

9. How do I know what to tithe on? My rule of thumb is this: Is it taxable income?

10. If it is taxable income, then I tithe on it. Does my business tithe? Again, is it taxable? I do not pay a tithe on the gross income of my business. I sow from my business as I want to, but that is not the tithe. If I pull money out of my business, then I tithe on what I take out of the business when I take it out of the business.

11. What if I do not have a church at the moment? You can tithe to whoever is feeding you spiritually until you find a church. Yes, many people do consider a distant church as their primary church through modern livestream and Facebook live broadcasts. If there is not a good Bible believing church in your town, you can tithe to a distant church. Many people in rural areas have made Faithlifechurch.org their home church because of that very thing.

Okay, let's move on.

The Lord showed me that most Christians give their tithe as a bill they owe (if they even tithe, and most do not). This means they exercise no faith in what they are doing but just know they owe the tithe and simply pay it as they would a bill.

While it is good to pay your tithe, you always want to pay your tithe in faith. Otherwise, your giving is being prompted from a legal standpoint instead of a faith-based viewpoint.

Let every word of God be revelation to you of God's intent toward you. The tithe is not a heavy weight to bear, and it should not be grievous to give it. God is not trying to *take* something from you, but rather, He is trying to *get* something to you. We are to believe and understand the benefit of the tithe and rejoice in it. The tithe is an act of worship that declares that God is our source. It has well-defined benefits that, when we tithe, we should be in faith to receive.

I always suggest a family already have their tithe made out when they come to church. I also suggest that, before they come to church, they lay their hands on that tithe, declare the benefit of it, and declare that the windows of heaven are open and that Satan is rebuked off of their harvest. They should also declare that Satan cannot steal from them and what they put their hands to will prosper, in the name of Jesus.

Now, lastly, let me wrap up our discussion of the tithe with a look at the tithe as recorded in the New Testament. Oh, yes, the tithe is mentioned there! The following passage is where we read from earlier.

> After Abram returned from defeating Kedorlaomer and the kings allied with him, the king of Sodom came out to meet him in the Valley of Shaveh (that is, the King's Valley). Then Melchizedek king of Salem brought out bread and wine. He was priest of God Most High, and he blessed Abram, saying, "Blessed be Abram by God Most High, Creator of heaven and earth. And praise be to God Most High, who delivered your enemies into your hand." *Then Abram gave him a tenth of everything.*
> —Genesis 14:17-20

Now, let's see what the writer of Hebrews says about the tithe.

> This Melchizedek was king of Salem and priest of God Most High. He met Abraham returning from the defeat of the kings and blessed him, and Abraham gave him a tenth of everything. First, the name Melchizedek means "king of righteousness"; then

also, "king of Salem" means "king of peace." Without father or mother, without genealogy, without beginning of days or end of life, resembling the Son of God, he remains a priest forever.

Just think how great he was: Even the patriarch Abraham gave him a tenth of the plunder! Now the law requires the descendants of Levi who become priests to collect a tenth from the people—that is, from their fellow Israelites—even though they also are descended from Abraham. This man, however, did not trace his descent from Levi, yet he collected a tenth from Abraham and blessed him who had the promises. And without doubt the lesser is blessed by the greater. In the one case, the tenth is collected by people who die; but in the other case, by him who is declared to be living.

—Hebrews 7:1-8

Please note that this text says, "*In the one case, the tenth is collected by people who die,*" referring to the Levites of the Old Testament. Then it goes on to say, "*But in the other case, by him **who is declared to be living**.*"

Melchizedek was the king of righteousness, king of peace, without mother or father, without beginning of days or end of life, resembling the Son of God, a priest forever. Melchizedek was Jesus Christ standing before Abraham that day. He was not known as Jesus at that moment however.

Remember, Joseph was told by the angel to name the baby boy Jesus when He was born. The name Jesus means Savior, thus indicating by His name who He was to be to us. Christ is not Jesus's last name. When we say Jesus Christ, we are literally saying the anointed Savior. Jesus was not known by the name Jesus when He stood before Abraham, because that plan was still being hidden from

Satan at that time.

So, the name Melchizedek was a name that simply reflected who He was, the King of Righteousness and the Prince of Peace. However, prophetically, Melchizedek was declaring Abraham's future by serving him bread and wine, which spoke of the new covenant (bread, His body broken for us, and the wine, His blood given for us) that would be made with the heirs of Abraham later on and would fulfill the promise that God gave to Abraham regarding his heirs in Genesis 12.

In regard to the tithe, Hebrews says the tithe is now collected by "him who is declared to be living." It is Jesus who now collects the tithe, the one who is declared to be living! He is the King of kings and the Lord of lords.

So, remember, the law of the tithe is still in effect today. The only thing that has changed is the priesthood. In the Old Testament, the tribe of Levi collected the tithe for the work of God. Today, Jesus (who came from the tribe of Judah, not Levi, indicating a new order of the priesthood was established) collects the tithe from His church for the work of the ministry. Of course, I realize that Jesus, the person, is not here personally collecting the tithe. But remember that the bible says the church is the body of Christ, meaning His legal expression here, just as our body gives us legal expression here. As we give to His church, His body, we are in fact giving to Jesus. The Levites, under the old covenant, collected the tithe on behalf of God's ministry then, and the church collects the tithe on behalf of God's ministry now.

THE TITHE IS A LEGAL FENCE AROUND YOUR LIFE THAT STOPS THE DEVIL FROM HAVING ACCESS TO STEAL YOUR PROVISION.

In review, the tithe is a legal fence around your life that stops the devil from having access to steal your provision. Remember, the tithe by itself does not cause you to prosper! Your prosperity is determined by what you do *inside* that fence!

The tithe is a law that is vital to your financial life. This is why I took so much time covering this important law of the Kingdom.

So, the next time you are at church and the pastor says it is time to receive the tithes, you should shout for joy, because now you know the benefits of the tithe.

CHAPTER 7
YOU NEED A PURSE: PART ONE

One of my best friends, Pastor Peter Mortlock, is a pastor at City Impact Church in Auckland, New Zealand. He has built an amazing ministry and has one of the largest churches in New Zealand.

Throughout our friendship over the years, we have probably done 20 or so motorcycle trips all over North America and New Zealand. He is the one that finally got me to buy a Harley. I was a Honda rider for years, but when we traveled, he always insisted I rent a Harley. At first, I did not like the Harley as much as my Honda, but if you know much about the Harley bike, they made some major changes to the design a few years ago, which I liked. So, this past year, Drenda bought me a brand-new Harley that we love to travel on.

During our rides, I noticed that Pastor Peter always had a leather bag—I called it a man purse—hanging around his shoulders. After getting sore from sitting on my wallet one day, I asked him about his bag. Well, that discussion led him to buy me one for my birthday. They are not as popular here in the states as they are in Europe and New Zealand, but I love it.

I usually always seemed to lose my sunglasses by setting them down somewhere and forgetting where I left them. But since I started using my man bag, or man purse, whatever you want to call it, I have never lost a pair. I totally understand now why the ladies love to carry purses. Everything is right there. It is awesome. Now, I am not trying to persuade you to buy a man purse, but I do want to suggest that you think about it.

Did you know that Jesus told us to carry a purse?

> *And do not set your heart on what you will eat or drink; do not worry about it. For the pagan world runs after all such things, and your Father knows that you need them. But seek his kingdom, and these things will be given to you as well.*
>
> *Do not be afraid, little flock, for your Father has been pleased to give you the kingdom. Sell your possessions and give to the poor. <u>Provide purses for yourselves</u> that will not wear out, a treasure in heaven that will never fail, where no thief comes near and no moth destroys. For where your treasure is, there your heart will be also.*
>
> —Luke 12:29-34

I do not think Jesus was pushing a fashion statement but, rather, a process that you need to understand. (And we can replace the word purse with wallet if you want.)

The point Jesus was trying to make was that you need an access point to your treasure.

For example, I could have a million dollars in the bank, but it does me no good if I cannot access it and use it, right? This is why you carry a wallet around with you—it is your access point to your assets.

Losing your wallet is one of the most stressful things that can happen. I always do my best to make sure that doesn't happen. My wallet, which is in my man purse, is always with me.

In these few words that I have quoted from Jesus, we find a ton of wisdom and key Kingdom principles in regard to your money in the Kingdom. First of all, the phrase "Do not worry" was used more than once. Jesus told us that God knows all about what we need and gave specific direction on how we can access His provision.

> *And do not set your heart on what you will eat or drink; <u>do not worry about it</u>. For the pagan world runs after all such things, and your Father knows that you need them. <u>But seek his kingdom</u>, and these things will be given to you as well.*

Jesus was saying not to worry because God has this covered; God knows what you need. But then Jesus inserted some instruction.

> *<u>But seek his kingdom</u>, and these things will be given to you as well.*

Jesus was saying that God has the answer, but there is a process to legally lay claim to it. God has the answer, BUT you need to know how the Kingdom works before you can lay claim to it.

Notice that Jesus did not say to seek God first but *the Kingdom*. I think most of us have interpreted that Scripture to mean seek God first, but it does not say that. Jesus made it very clear. If just seeking God was the answer, He would have said, "So seek *God*, and all these things will be given to you." God knows what you need, but there is a legal process that must take place before what heaven has can legally be transferred to you here in the earth realm.

Let me remind you that the Kingdom of God is a government with a King. The King's authority and will is carried down to every citizen of the Kingdom through the administration of the laws of the Kingdom.

Throughout my previous four books on the Kingdom, I took the time to review the aspects of Kingdom life, faith, and jurisdiction. Why? Because these principles are absolutely vital to your success and understanding of Kingdom life. I have reviewed these key components of the Kingdom in all of my books, knowing that many may pick up any one book and need to know the foundational knowledge of what actually changed my life.

You need to learn how the Kingdom operates!

Information in this chapter has been taken from my other books in the Your Financial Revolution series. If you have read them, you are free to move on to chapter eight. If you have not read them, or want to review these basic and vital principles of the Kingdom, stay right here with me in chapter seven.

The jurisdiction issue

As I stated earlier, I live out in the country on 60 acres of some of the prettiest land in Ohio. I originally had 55 acres, but my neighbor sold me a piece of land that bordered my land to bring my total up to 60 acres. We have surely enjoyed this land over the last 22 years. Having woods to hunt deer, a marsh to hunt ducks, and fields to hunt rabbits and pheasants, as well as to run around in on our four wheelers, is just a blessing.

If you took a close look at my place, you would find NO TRESPASSING signs on the perimeter of the property. The signs are there so people will know where my property line begins. The law in Ohio says that a person who wants to be on my land must have a written consent form on them at all times when they are on the property. If they do not, they are considered to be trespassing, and they legally can be thrown off and could incur penalties and fines in the process.

So in brief...

You cannot occupy something you do not have legal jurisdiction over.

So as I said, having a written consent form, signed by me, would give you legal access to my property. If someone stopped you on my property and they asked you why you were there and you replied that I had told you that you could hunt there, that would not be good enough. The law says that you must have a signed form to have access.

This same process is needed if you went to the bank and demanded your money; they would ask to see your identification (ID). A retail clerk has the same right to ask for your identification when you use a credit card to pay for merchandise. The presentation of an ID is not meant to hinder you from your accounts; it is to protect you from others fraudulently accessing your stuff.

> LEARN WHAT IS YOURS AND HOW TO ACCESS IT. THEN ALL THESE THINGS THAT YOU NEED WILL BE ADDED TO YOU.

When Jesus said to seek first the Kingdom, He was actually saying, "*Study the laws of the Kingdom to know how to operate legally and effectively within your legal rights as a citizen of the Kingdom.*" Learn what is yours and how to access it. Then all these things that you need will be added to you.

Another example would be if I had a trust fund for my son. Once he became of age and it was legal to transfer the account to him, I would have to tell him what bank it was in, show him how to make withdrawals from the account, and how to make deposits back into the account. Even though it was legally his account, he would still be held accountable to the legal process of the law to access it.

Let me summarize what I am saying here. When Jesus said to

seek the Kingdom, He was saying to learn how the Kingdom works, referring to the laws and processes in the Kingdom that you must learn to legally lay hold of what is already yours. So as we have seen in my bank account example, you may have legal jurisdiction over an asset but yet may not occupy it because you were not able to follow the legal process to actually occupy it. For instance, if you left your ID at home when you went to the bank, they would not allow you to take money out of an account even though it was your money.

Understanding the jurisdiction issue in the Kingdom is a prerequisite to operating effectively in the Kingdom.

I am sure you have probably heard a story like this: Someone who is well known gets sick, and prayer is called for them. Millions of people join in prayer on behalf of this person's healing, and yet they die. Why?

Or someone tells you that their grandmother died even though they were praying for them, and they want to know why. Or someone tells you that they have sown money for a financial need, and yet they continue to be broke. Are there answers for these types of questions?

Before I answer that, let's acknowledge that we do not know everything that is going on in the spirit realm, and I am not pretending that I do. However, based on the Word of God, we know that if someone is sick, Jesus already paid the price for their healing. We know that if we are generous and give, the Bible says we shall receive. Yet on a daily basis, we see what looks like the apparent failure of the Word of God to function as it is written in many people's lives. Is God the one who is to blame?

As I discuss this topic in this chapter, you will find the answer to be a resounding NO. If no, then what is the problem? After all, most people blame God for tragedies. They know He has the power to stop bad things from happening and He didn't, so they assume He *chose* not to. This is where the faulty doctrine that says "God allows bad things to happen to good people" comes from. People believe that if He did not stop it or intervene, He must have allowed it. But if you have the understanding that God is always good and He cannot lie, you would know the problem must not lie with God, Himself but somewhere else; and you would begin a quest to find the answer.

Just as when you walk into a room and it is dark, you do not automatically claim the power company has failed you. No, you find the switch, and if that does not work, you check the bulb. You have an understanding that, most likely, the issue is on *your* end.

If you had the knowledge that it could *never* be God's fault, as He has given us His Word and promises that reveal His will toward us, then you would begin a diligent search for the short circuit that cut off God's answer.

The disciples demonstrated this mindset when they could not cast the demon out of the boy in Matthew 17:14-23. Instead of asking, "Why did God choose to leave that demon there?" they asked Jesus, "Why couldn't *we* cast it out?" This should be our immediate question when circumstances seem to contradict the Word of God.

So again, it is vital that we must, first, know that God is good and, second, that He does not lie. You must read the Bible and ask questions if you want to learn how the Kingdom works. Remember, those great Bible stories are there for a reason—Jesus is trying to show you something.

Again, the Kingdom of God is a kingdom and operates with laws and principles that never change. Those principles, as I said, can be learned and used just as a farmer understands the laws of seedtime and harvest in the earth realm and uses those laws to prosper. Because the Kingdom operates by laws, which are given to every citizen to understand and use in the Kingdom, *anyone* can learn them.

Sometimes, knowing how these laws work can be life and death.

Mark and Hannah came to our church and desired to have a baby. Up until that time, Hannah was told by doctors that due to various issues in her body, it would be almost impossible for her to get pregnant or to carry a baby. But while hearing about the goodness of God and learning Kingdom law at Faith Life Church, she found out she was pregnant. She was thrilled beyond words. But before long, she began to have severe pain in her abdomen, a couple of times so severe that she passed out.

After one of these episodes, Hannah wanted to have things checked out, so she went to her doctor's office. Her doctor was not in, but the doctor on call wanted to do an ultrasound to see what was going on.

The doctor saw a large blood clot and told her that she had miscarried. There was no heartbeat.

The doctor offered to have her come in the following day so she could remove the dead baby from her womb, but Hannah refused. Instead, her husband, Mark, encouraged her with the Word of God and God's promises and encouraged her not to cast aside her confidence in the Word of God concerning the baby.

That weekend, Hannah received prayer at church and was convinced that she would have a healthy baby in spite of what the doctor had told her.

That Monday, she went in to see her personal doctor as her doctor was not in the day she had stopped by the office. Her doctor suggested that she have another ultrasound. The doctor seemed shocked as she stared at the ultrasound screen and immediately looked at the scans that were done a few days earlier. Then she said the following words to Hannah. "I have been doing this for 30 years, and I have never seen this happen before. I can see the big blood clot on last week's scans and the absence of a heartbeat. As I look at you today, the entire blood clot is gone, and there is a perfect baby alive with a perfect heartbeat."

A few months later, Hannah gave birth to a perfect baby girl, who she named Evelyn. Curious one day as to the meaning of the name Evelyn, she looked it up and was surprised to discover that the name actually means *life*! As I write this today, Hannah's second baby is due any day now.

This amazing story was obviously the work of God. But as a spiritual scientist, you should be thinking of a few questions right now, like: "Why did it happen? Is Hannah one of God's favorites? Did God just randomly choose to heal her baby?" Those are questions that must be answered.

Again, to the average Christian, a miracle has taken place. But I encourage people to rethink the word "miracle," as it implies something out of the ordinary. In the Kingdom, however, this was simply a function of Kingdom law.

If I dropped a rock and it fell to the ground, you would think I was nuts if I yelled out, "WOW, did you see that? The rock just fell to the ground! That's a miracle!" You would disagree that it was a miracle because you know the action was simply the function of the law of gravity, and it works the same way *every time* for *anyone*. The rock will *always* fall to the ground.

So, as spiritual scientists, we must look for clues as to what happened, spiritual clues that will reveal the law or laws of the Kingdom that were present in the story.

One of the greatest stories in the Bible that will help us find some answers concerning faith and jurisdiction is found in Luke chapter 8.

As Jesus was on his way, the crowds almost crushed him. And a woman was there who had been subject to bleeding for twelve years, but no one could heal her. She came up behind him and touched the edge of his cloak, and immediately her bleeding stopped.

"Who touched me?" Jesus asked.

When they all denied it, Peter said, "Master, the people are crowding and pressing against you."

But Jesus said, "Someone touched me; I know that power has gone out from me."

Then the woman, seeing that she could not go unnoticed, came trembling and fell at his feet. In the presence of all the people, she told why she had touched him and how she had been instantly healed. Then he said to her, "<u>Daughter, your faith has healed you</u>. Go in peace."

—Luke 8:42b-48

In this story, we find a woman who was very sick for many years and could not get well. Coming up behind Jesus, she touched His cloak and was immediately healed. Now, there are some very profound clues to the Kingdom's operation in this story that we can learn from and that will bring to light some of the answers we are looking for.

First of all, the people in the crowd that was surrounding Jesus were all touching Him, as the story says He was almost being crushed by the crowd pressing against Him. When Jesus asked, "Who touched me?" Peter was amazed at the question because, again, *everyone* was touching him. But Jesus said this particular person had touched Him in a different way—He had felt the power of the Holy Spirit flow out of Him.

After reading this story, all kinds of bells and whistles should be going off in your spirit urging you to stop and consider what just happened. Your mind should have immediately launched into investigative mode with a myriad of questions. As spiritual scientists, we need to know why *this* woman was healed and no one else was. I assume there were many others there who were physically touching Him and were also sick, yet they were not healed. So, we need to ask, "Why did the anointing flow only to this woman and not to everyone else who touched Jesus at that moment?"

The traditional religious answer is that she was healed because Jesus healed her. But did He? Was Jesus intentionally ministering to her when she was healed? Had he laid His hands on her? Did He command the sickness to leave her body? The answer is no. In fact, Jesus did not even know she was there. He had to ask who had touched Him.

So, did Jesus actually choose to heal her at that moment? Again, He did not even know she was there. So how was she healed? Why was she healed? As spiritual scientists, we can rule out the thought that she was one of God's special children or that she had a special connection to Jesus, because Acts 10:34 says that God is no respecter of persons.

We can also assume that since Jesus did not even know she was there, He had no part in her decision to be healed that day. We can agree that He was the reservoir of the anointing, but He was not part of the decision *she* made to be healed at that moment.

Jesus tells us exactly how she tapped into the Kingdom's authority and power. He said, "*Daughter, your faith has healed you. Go in peace.*" This sentence tells us everything we need to know and answers our question as to why and how she received that day. As spiritual scientists, let's begin to take a closer look at this story and see if we can pick up on any clues as to why she received her healing.

First of all, Jesus calls her *daughter*, meaning she was part of the nation of Israel, a descendant of Abraham. As a child of Abraham, she possessed the blessing given to Abraham and the benefits of the covenant that God made with Abraham.

> *He said, "If you listen carefully to the Lord your God and do what is right in his eyes, if you pay attention to his commands and keep all his decrees, I will not bring on you any of the diseases I brought on the Egyptians, for I am the Lord, who heals you."*
> —Exodus 15:26

So when Jesus called her daughter, that meant she had a legal right to all that was included in Abraham's covenant he made with God. But this fact alone cannot be the only reason she received, as everyone there that day that was pressing against Jesus had that same legality. There had to be something else that caused the power of the Kingdom of God to flow. Jesus then tells us one more reason she received. In fact, Jesus said this was the *exact* reason she personally received.

He said *her faith* had healed her.

So now we know the reason she was able to receive—it was her legal right to receive since she was a daughter of Abraham, and her faith was the switch that allowed that power to flow personally into her body at that exact moment.

The fact that she was a daughter can be compared to the power company having the power on and the wires coming into your home. The power is available, but that does not mean your lights will be on. You must also flip the switch to on before the lights will come on.

So, as a legal descendent of Abraham, this woman had a legal right to be healed. However, because she had jurisdiction on the earth and over her own life, she had to personally turn on the switch to release that power.

But where is the switch? How do we turn it on?

To find out, we need to define our terms.

What is faith?

Faith is a term that Christians throw around loosely, and I am convinced that many, if not the majority, do not know what faith actually is, why it is needed, how to know if they are in faith, and how to obtain faith. If faith is the switch that allowed the anointing to flow and heal this woman, then we need to take a very close look at faith!

We find our definition of faith in Romans 4.

> *Against all hope, Abraham in hope believed and so became the father of many nations, just as it had been said to him, "So shall your offspring be." Without weakening in his faith, he faced the fact that his body was as good as dead—since he was about a hundred years old—and that Sarah's womb was also dead. Yet he did not waver through unbelief regarding the promise of God, but was strengthened in his faith and gave glory to God, <u>being fully persuaded</u> that God had power to do what he had promised.*
> —Romans 4:18-21

Let's understand the setting of this story. Abraham and Sarah could not have children. I do not mean they were having trouble conceiving a child and should have kept trying. I mean they were almost 100 years old, and it was over. Their bodies could not have children; it was impossible! Yet God promised Abraham a child even though in the natural, it was utterly impossible.

The Bible says that Abraham was *fully persuaded* that God had the power to do what He said in spite of the natural facts that stated a different story. Here then is our definition of faith: being fully persuaded that God has the power to do what He has promised.

I state it this way: "**Your heart being in agreement with heaven**." Not just agreeing mentally with what God says but being *fully persuaded.*

Our definition of what faith is

Say it out loud with me to be sure you get it: Faith is being fully persuaded of what God says. It is our hearts and minds being in agreement with heaven, *fully persuaded.*

Why is faith needed?

Why can't God heal everyone in the hospital when He wants to? Why can't He stop wars? Why can't He send angels to preach the Gospel to us? I am sure you have heard all of these questions before. The answer is that He can't.

It is not that God does not have the *power* to do so. He does not have the *jurisdiction* to do so.

To understand what I am saying, we need to look at Hebrews.

> *But there is a place where someone has testified:*
> *"What is mankind that you are mindful of them, a son of man that you care for him? You made them a little lower than the angels; you crowned them with glory and honor and put everything under their feet."*
> *In putting everything under them, God left nothing that*

is not subject to them. Yet at present we do not see everything subject to them.

—Hebrews 2:6-8

God gave man complete legal jurisdiction over the entire earth realm when he was placed here. There was nothing that was not under his jurisdiction. He ruled over this realm with absolute jurisdiction and authority. His ability to rule with authority was backed up by the government that had set him here. In essence, he ruled with the delegated authority of the Kingdom of God. He wore the crown of that government, which represented the glory of God, the anointing, and the position of honor or authority that he bore.

Now, of course, he did not really wear a literal metal crown, but he did have a crown in the sense of what a crown speaks of. To get a good picture of what this looks like, think of a natural king. Although he is a natural man and bears no real power in his natural being, he wears a crown, which signifies he stands in representation of not only himself but also of an entire kingdom and government. His words carry authority only because they are backed up by all

HEAVEN HAS NO JURISDICTION ON THE EARTH UNLESS A MAN OR WOMAN'S HEART IS FULLY PERSUADED OF WHAT HEAVEN SAYS, WHICH IS CALLED FAITH.

the power and natural resources of the government and the kingdom he represents.

If you think of a sheriff directing traffic, he will stop a massive tractor-trailer truck with just a few words, "Stop, in the name of the law!"

Yes, the truck is much bigger than the man, and the man, in himself, is no match for the truck. But the truck stops not because of the man but because of the badge the man wears, which represents a government that backs him. In this case, the government is much bigger than the man who wears the badge. For the truck driver, there is no fear of the *man*, but there is a fear of the government which the man represents, so he stops the truck. The same is true here. Adam ruled over everything that was created in the earth realm. God's power and dominion, represented by the crown of glory and honor, gave man the assurance that his words ruled on behalf of the Kingdom of God.

> *The highest heavens belong **to** the Lord, but the earth he has **given to mankind.***
>
> —Psalm 115:16

This principle of man's jurisdiction over the earth is vital to your understanding of Kingdom law, especially why faith is required for God to gain legal jurisdiction in a situation.

> *Jesus said to them, "A prophet is not without honor except in his own town, among his relatives and in his own home." **He could not do any miracles there**, except lay his hands on a few sick people and heal them. He was amazed at their lack of faith.*
>
> —Mark 6:4-6

If I asked people on the street if Jesus could do anything, they would probably say He could. If I then asked if there was any place in the Bible where Jesus tried but could not do miracles, what would they say?

I assure you they would tell me that there was no such place in the Bible, yet you just read one. Jesus could not heal them. As a spiritual scientist, I want to know why.

The answer is simply—He couldn't, and now you know it was because they had no faith, no agreement with heaven, and thus heaven had no legal jurisdiction in that situation.

Make sure you have a clear understanding of what we have discovered.

Heaven has no jurisdiction on the earth unless a man or woman's heart is fully persuaded of what heaven says, which is called FAITH.

As in our earlier example, let's assume that someone you knew was sick, and they were well known around the world. Millions were asked to pray for them and they did, but the person died anyway. Did the Word of God fail? No. That's impossible. So, we must find our answer somewhere else.

> *And when you pray, do not keep on babbling like pagans, for they think they will be heard because of their many words. Do not be like them, for your Father knows what you need before you ask him.*
>
> —Matthew 6:7-8

A lot of people believe that the more people that are praying, the greater chance of God hearing and being moved to help. I hope I have covered enough by now that you know this is completely false. And when I say there was no faith, primarily, I am talking about the one who needs to receive from God having faith. You would have to agree that Jesus had plenty of faith in our story out of Mark chapter 6, yet He could not heal them.

So if you and I were talking about the sick friend with millions praying for them, I would ask you, "What is *he* (the sick friend) *saying?*"

We could have 20 *billion* people praying for someone, but if the sick person is saying he or she is going to die, he or she will die.

Again, let's consider our example we just looked at in Mark 6. We know that Jesus had faith to heal, but He could not do anything for the people without their faith being engaged.

I have had numerous people come to me stating that their grandmother or their grandfather or a relative was sick and say that they had been praying for them, yet nothing was happening. I always ask, "What is the grandmother saying? What is the grandfather saying? Is there faith there?"

You see, you do not have spiritual authority over another person. You can minister to them, but they have to be engaged in that. One thing I tell people to do when I am praying for them is to change the picture. I am talking about the picture they see about their own situation in their minds. I want to change that picture from death to life.

> John's disciples told him about all these things. Calling two of them, he sent them to the Lord to ask, "Are you the one who is to come, or should we expect someone else?"
>
> When the men came to Jesus, they said, "John the Baptist sent us to you to ask, 'Are you the one who is to come, or should we expect someone else?'"
>
> At that very time Jesus cured many who had diseases, sicknesses and evil spirits, and gave sight to many who were blind. So he replied to the messengers, "Go back and report to John what you have seen and heard: The blind receive sight, the lame walk,

*those who have leprosy are cleansed, the deaf hear, the dead are
raised, and the good news is proclaimed to the poor.*
—Luke 7:18-22

Notice Jesus did not refer to a Scripture. He could have said,
"You go back and tell John this Scripture or that Scripture." But
no, He told them to tell John about all of the good things that were
happening by the power and authority of the Kingdom of God.

To help a friend or family member, you would do the same.
Tell your friend who is sick a story of how Jesus healed someone
else. If possible, tell them a story about someone that was healed
from the exact same disease that is afflicting their body. Giving them
that picture will inspire them and bring hope. Hope always carries a
picture with it, and this is the picture you want your friend or family
member to see, that there is healing for that disease.

Once your friend or family member sees that it is possible to
be healed, they will then ask you how that is possible. This is the
moment you have been waiting for—they are now open to receiving
instruction regarding the Word of God and the principles of the
Kingdom. You will want to bring them into the Kingdom if they
are not born again first, and secondly, spend some time with them
explaining the Scriptures regarding healing. If possible, leave them
some material to reinforce what you have told them. We have seen
multiplied hundreds of people healed of every kind of disease and
set free by doing this. Another thing I do, before praying for them,
is to ask them why they think they will be healed when we pray. I
want their faith to be anchored to a Scripture, not simply the action
of praying.

We now know what faith is—agreement with heaven, your heart
fully persuaded of what God says. We also now understand that faith

is required to give God legal jurisdiction in the earth through the person that is in agreement with heaven.

How do we get in faith?

Consequently, faith comes from hearing the message, and the message is heard through the word about Christ.

—Romans 10:17

How does faith come by hearing the Word of God? What is the process? Is just hearing the Word all it takes for faith to be developed in the human spirit?

To understand how faith comes and what Romans 10:17 is talking about, we can look to Mark chapter 4. I always say if you throw your Bible up in the air, it should land open to Mark chapter 4; it is that important!

Jesus said in Mark 4:13 that if you did not understand what He was teaching in this parable you would not be able to understand *any other* parable in the Bible. I would say that is pretty important! Why is this chapter so important? Because it tells us how heaven interfaces with the earth realm, how it gains jurisdiction, and where that takes place. Nothing is more important to your life than knowing what this whole chapter is talking about.

In this chapter, Jesus tells us three parables regarding how faith is produced in the human spirit, which is, as you know now, a requirement for heaven to legally invade Earth. The three stories in this chapter are the parable of the sower, the parable of the man scattering seed, and the story of the mustard seed.

Let's start by looking at the second story Jesus tells in Mark chapter 4, the story of the man scattering seed.

He also said, "This is what the kingdom of God is like. A man scatters seed on the ground. Night and day, whether he sleeps or gets up, the seed sprouts and grows, though he does not know how. All by itself the soil produces grain—first the stalk, then the head, then the full kernel in the head. As soon as the grain is ripe, he puts the sickle to it, because the harvest has come."

—Mark 4:26-29

The first thing we need to do is to define our terms. What is the *seed* Jesus is talking about, and what is the ground? Jesus actually defines those two terms in the preceding parable of the sower in the same chapter.

The seed is the Word of God, and the ground is the heart of man, or the spirit of man. So in this parable, Jesus says a man scatters the Word of God into his heart. Then, *all by itself*, the soil, or the *heart* of man, starts to produce faith or agreement with heaven. This is the natural process and function of your human spirit—it is going to incubate what you put in there.

Before I go forward, it is critical that you remember what our definition of faith is—*the heart of a man or a woman fully persuaded of what heaven says.*

The thing to remember here is that agreement with heaven is not the same thing as mentally agreeing with the Word of God. The Bible says that Abraham was *fully persuaded*. To help you get a clear picture of what fully persuaded looks and feels like, let's say I told you to jump from the top of the Empire State building in New York City. To convince you to try it, I told you that if you flapped your arms hard enough, you could fly safely down to Earth. You would laugh in my face, because you KNOW what would happen to you. You are fully persuaded of the result. That is what fully persuaded feels like. You *know*, you are persuaded, there is no other possibly—you would die if you jumped.

So, let's take another situation and see how you do with it. Let's assume that you have a very visible, large lump in your body, and the doctor says you have just one month left to live. You have cancer. In fact, the doctor says that your form of cancer is so rare that there is no one that has actually lived that has been diagnosed with it.

Now, let's assume you know what 1 Peter 2:24 says.

> *"He himself bore our sins" in his body on the cross, so that we might die to sins and live for righteousness; "by his wounds you have been healed."*
>
> —1 Peter 2:24

The Scripture tells us the answer, but you and I have a serious problem: We grew up in the kingdom of darkness, and perversion and death are all around us. We have grown up in the kingdom of fear and have been fully persuaded of what fear says. So, in the above illustration, we have been trained that cancer can kill. We have evidence in every media broadcast that this is true. So how are we going to change our agreement? How can we become fully persuaded of what God says? Well, in reality, we can't by ourselves. But the Word of God is alive and full of power, and by planting it in your spirit, all by itself, your spirit and the Word begin to produce agreement with what heaven says.

> *He also said, "This is what the kingdom of God is like. A man scatters seed on the ground. Night and day, whether he sleeps or gets up, the seed sprouts and grows, though he does not know how. **All by itself the soil produces grain**—first the stalk, then*

the head, then the full kernel in the head. As soon as the grain is ripe, he puts the sickle to it, because the harvest has come."
—Mark 4:26-29

All by itself, the soil, (your heart) produces agreement. Notice you cannot pray for faith; it is a function of your heart and the Word. As we look at this text, we can see that the agreement of our hearts and heaven is a process. It does not happen instantly. This illustration tells us that, at first, when our hearts receive the Word, faith starts to grow just like a blade or sprout of a newly planted seed grows. It then continues to grow into a stalk, and then it forms a head. The head is where the seed, or fruit, begins to form. At this phase of the plant's life, you still have nothing to eat. The plant has not produced its mature, ripe fruit yet, but it is growing.

So it is with the Word of God. There is no visible change yet in the natural realm when faith is growing. There is not agreement yet, but be assured the plant *is* growing, faith *is* being produced, and agreement *is* happening. Jesus goes on to explain that when the seed in the head is fully mature, or ripe, the harvest has come, agreement is there, and now faith is there.

When you plant a seed in the ground, through the process of germination, the plant starts to grow, but there is no fruit yet. The plant continues growing as long as it stays in the right environment. As it matures, it shoots out its fruit.

Let's say you are growing corn. The corn plant shoots out a corn ear, but at first, it is just a small ear of corn with no ripe corn that you could eat. But after a season, the corn on the ear becomes mature and ripe. Catch this point! At the moment the kernel of corn on the ear matches the kernel of corn that was sown into the ground, there is agreement.

When the seed that is in head of the plant matures, it will look exactly—EXACTLY—like the seed that was sown.

Plant a corn plant, and the mature seed in the ear will match the seed that you planted. They are the same. They look the same and taste the same so much so that you could not tell them apart.

So let me paraphrase what Jesus is saying. When we hear the Word of God (Romans 10:17), we are actually scattering God's Word into our spirit men, our hearts. If we keep that Word in our hearts, it will grow and mature; and when it is mature, our hearts will be fully persuaded of what heaven says. Heaven and earth match, and heaven has now gained legal jurisdiction in the earth realm through the person that is fully persuaded. Our thoughts and belief exactly match what heaven says with full confidence. This is not a mental thing. This has now become what we actually believe just as sure as we believe a rock will fall if dropped. Heaven sows the Word from heaven into the earth realm where it will bring about agreement and God's will. If heaven says you are healed, then when that Word matures in your heart, all you will see is what heaven says. No more fear. When you close your eyes, you will see yourself healed! This is why Hebrews 11:1 (KJV) says,

> *Now faith is the substance of things hoped for, the <u>evidence of things not seen</u>.*

You may not see it yet in the natural, but you have seen it in your spirit; and it is just as real as if you were holding it in your hand. That agreement is called faith, and that faith will bring that picture to pass here in the earth realm, in your life!

But this is not where Mark chapter 4 stops. After it teaches us how our hearts come into agreement with heaven and faith is there, it gives us instruction on how to harvest that fruit.

> *As soon as the grain is ripe, __he puts the sickle to it__, because the harvest has come.*
>
> —Mark 4:29

Notice that even though the heart is in agreement with heaven and there is faith, nothing happens yet. Why? As I have been saying all along, you have the legal jurisdiction here in the earth realm.

Do you remember our discussion about Luke 8 regarding the woman with the issue of blood? Remember, Jesus says, "Daughter, *your* faith has healed you." I told you then that when Jesus used the word "daughter," He inferred a legal standing before heaven. She was a daughter of Abraham. She had legal rights. I compared it to having the wires from the power plant connected to your house. The power is there and available, but you still have to personally turn on the lights. In the same way, once faith is established, the power is available, but nothing happens until you turn the switch on.

YOU have to release the power of the Kingdom of God here in the earth realm, because only you, a man or woman on the earth, can legally do it. This principle is exactly how you were saved, as mentioned in Romans 10:10.

> *For it is with your heart that you believe and are justified, and it is with your mouth that you profess your faith and are saved.*
>
> —Romans 10:10

With the heart, man believes the Word and is justified. Justify is a legal term meaning the administration of law. So, when a man or woman's heart is in agreement with heaven— when they believe what heaven says—they are justified before heaven and Earth. It is now legal for heaven to flow *into* their lives and *through* their lives and impact the earth on behalf of the Kingdom of God. But strangely, even though it is now legal and they are in faith, still nothing happens. "But, Gary, I thought you said if I was in faith, it gave heaven legal jurisdiction here." Correct, but someone has to release heaven's authority here once faith exists. Let's look at our Scripture one more time.

> For it is with your heart that you believe and are justified, **and it is with your mouth that you profess your faith and are saved**.
>
> —Romans 10:10

Once you are in faith, or justified, it is now legal for heaven to invade Earth. But notice that it then says that it is with *your mouth* that you confess and are saved. Do you see the two parts? Heaven's part is bringing the Word into your heart where it incubates agreement here in the earth realm. Then, once agreement, or faith, is there, you

ONCE YOU ARE IN FAITH, OR JUSTIFIED, IT IS NOW LEGAL FOR HEAVEN TO INVADE EARTH.

must act on that agreement and release the authority of heaven into your situation to actually receive what heaven says.

In our Scripture in Mark 4, it says when the harvest is come, the man (on the earth) puts the sickle in. He is the one that has to act on the Word of God once faith is there and actually receive that harvest.

Let me go back and talk about the sickle referenced in Mark 4 for a moment. I believe that most of the church world has not been taught how to use the sickle, meaning they have not been taught how to harvest what they need. I did not know this either until the Lord began teaching me how the Kingdom operated. My first revelation of this vital process in the Kingdom happened years ago when I was invited to speak at a Wednesday night service at a church in Atlanta.

The church was not that big, but that was fine with me. I just love teaching people about the Kingdom. As I arrived at the church, I found it strange that the doors were locked and no one was there. It was only ten minutes before service was to begin.

I heard a really loud truck behind me, and I looked over to see an old pickup truck pulling in behind the alley of the church. I thought nothing of it. After all, I was in downtown Atlanta.

As I waited, a man came walking from behind the building and introduced himself as the pastor. He said he was sorry for being late, but his old truck would not start. He told me he had to start it by rolling it down a hill as the clutch was out. He went on to say that sometimes it would not start at all, and he would be forced to walk the five miles to church.

I will have to admit that I was a little surprised by this conversation. He went on to explain that his ministry really was primarily an outreach ministry and that he fed thousands of people every month, often over 10,000 meals a month from that one location.

As the pastor was speaking, I was getting upset. Here was a man of God who was feeding 10,000 people a month, and he did not even have a decent car? I could take care of that. I had a fairly new car with 20,000 miles on it at home that I would give him.

I told him of my plan and that I would send one of my staff down to Atlanta with the car. Of course, he was thrilled. I spent that night teaching him and his small church about the Kingdom of God and how it functioned in relation to money. I knew it was vital that they begin to demonstrate what the Kingdom looked like to those who so desperately needed it.

When I went home, I arranged for the car to be driven to Atlanta. When my staff member came to pick up the car, I knew that I was making a spiritual transaction in heaven. I knew that as I released that car into the Kingdom of God, I could believe God for a vehicle that I would have need of as well.

I am not a car person, meaning I am not really into cars. Some people are, but I am not. So I laid my hand on that car as my staff member came to pick it up, and I basically said, "Father, I release this car into this assignment in Atlanta. As I release it, I sow it as a seed and believe that I receive a…." I could not think of a car that I wanted, so I said, "I will get back to you on that!"

Well, over the next couple of months, I really did not think much about a car, but one morning I asked Drenda what kind of car she would like to have. After she thought for a bit, she said that a convertible would be nice. I asked her what kind of convertible she wanted, and neither of us could think of any models that were out there. Since I was buying the car for Drenda, I wanted to be sure that she got the car she liked, so I told her to check online or look around and let me know if she found a convertible she would like. Meanwhile, we did not tell anyone about our desire for a new car, but we kept our eyes open as we drove around looking for a car that might catch our attention.

One day we were pulling into a local restaurant for lunch, and, suddenly, Drenda yelled out, "There it is!"

"There what is?" I asked.

"The car I like." She pointed across the parking lot. I drove around the lot and pulled in behind a BMW 6 series Ci convertible, a beautiful car for sure. And might I add an expensive car as well. I complimented her on her taste and told her that it was a beautiful car.

Now, you need to know that Drenda and I do not go out and pay big bucks for cars. As I said, I have never really been a car guy. Being in finance, I also know how fast they depreciate and that it is always best to buy a car that is one to two years old. So that was my plan, to look for a great used one.

A week later, a guy from the church called me and said, "I found Drenda's car!" I was puzzled as we had not told anyone about the BMW we saw that day at lunch.

I asked him what kind of car it was, and he said it was a BMW 6 series Ci convertible. He said as he was driving around, he saw it, and the Lord told him it was Drenda's car.

"Okay, now you have my attention," I told him. The car was just a year old and in mint condition. I ended up paying cash for it. Drenda got her car. How did that happen? Let's compare the story to what we learned about being in faith and putting the sickle in.

When I gave my car away, I was in faith. But when Drenda said out loud, "That's it!" she was putting the sickle in, and a few days later the car showed up.

Although I heard her say out loud, "That's it!" I never tied her declaration to Mark chapter 4 and the sickle. But this next story made it crystal clear.

I've mentioned a few times that I own 60 acres of land. About 10 acres of the land is marsh. I love to hunt in the fall, but even though I had hunted ducks back in high school, I really had not done any duck hunting here in Ohio. One year, though, the marsh was full of water, and the ducks just kept flying into it in big flocks. Hundreds a day would be coming in to roost at night. So I grabbed my shotgun one night and went out and had a great time shooting a few ducks for dinner. That fall, both my boys and I enjoyed some good duck hunting.

One thing I noticed, however, was that a lot of the time, the ducks were at my maximum shotgun range. When hunting ducks, legally, you are only allowed to use steel shot as opposed to the traditional lead shot. Lead shot is heavier and retains its energy much farther out then steel shot, thus the problem with shooting long-range shots while duck hunting. But during that fall, as I was talking to a few fellow duck hunters, they told me about these new guns that were designed just for duck hunting. They were able to shoot heavier shot loads and were camouflaged as well. I was very interested in possibly buying one, but it was December and duck season was closing, so I did not think much more about it.

I happened to stop by Cabela's, our local sporting goods store, in early January for something, and I remembered those duck guns. I wanted to see one. So, I walked past the gun counter on the way out, and I saw a complete section of new guns dedicated to waterfowl hunting. I remember, without thinking about it, pointing my finger at the one I thought looked the best and saying out loud. "Lord, I will have that one." I did not think about it as I said it; it just came out of my mouth. The duck season did not open again until fall, so I was not planning to buy the gun until the season got a little closer.

Two weeks later, I was invited to speak at a business conference. As I finished, the CEO came out to thank me and said they had a gift for me. Amazingly, he brought out the exact gun—*the exact model*—I had pointed at two weeks earlier in Cabela's. Of course, I was totally surprised by such a generous gift, but I also knew it was not a coincidence. I remembered what I had said at Cabela's and realized what I had done. I had put the sickle in!

Understanding what you have just read in this chapter is, as I said before, *vital* to you being able to receive anything and everything from God. Everything you receive from God will go through this same process, so make sure you understand what you have just read. Reread it if you need to! It is that important!

CHAPTER 8
YOU NEED A PURSE: PART TWO

We had to take that long detour because I know it is essential for you to get a grasp on what the Kingdom is all about. Again, most Christians have no understanding of the legal operation of the Kingdom in the earth realm, and they have no understanding of the legal standing they personally possess in the Kingdom either. Now you know why I had to take that detour into the topics of faith and jurisdiction. Because without that basic understanding, you would have no idea what our Scripture here in Luke is talking about when it says to seek first the Kingdom and all these things will be added to you.

Now that you know what that means, let's go back to our text.

> *And do not set your heart on what you will eat or drink; do not worry about it. For the pagan world runs after all such things, and your Father knows that you need them. <u>But seek his kingdom, and these things will be given to you as well.</u>*
>
> *Do not be afraid, little flock, for your Father has been pleased to give you the kingdom. Sell your possessions and give to the poor. <u>Provide purses for yourselves</u> that will not wear out, a treasure in heaven that will never fail, where no thief comes*

near and no moth destroys. For where your treasure is, there your
heart will be also.

—Luke 12:29-34

Again, the Father already knows what you need, and everything you need has already been provided by the Father and is already yours, but you have to know and understand the legal process of receiving from heaven to enjoy all that He has.

Verse 32 lays out the incredible inheritance you have received as a son or daughter of the King. He says, "***Your Father has been pleased to give you the kingdom.***"

The Spirit itself beareth witness with our spirit, that we are
the children of God: And if children, then heirs; heirs of God,
and joint-heirs with Christ; if so be that we suffer with him, that
we may be also glorified together.

—Romans 8:16-17 (KJV)

Paul says we are joint heirs with Christ. As a son or daughter, you have an inheritance, the Kingdom.

Stop and think about that for a moment. You already legally have a right to all the Kingdom has in it. You don't have to beg. It is already yours.

Oh, how I hope you really grab hold of that statement. This is why 2 Corinthians 1:20 says the following:

For no matter how many promises God has made, they are
"Yes" in Christ. And so through him the "Amen" is spoken by us
to the glory of God.

—2 Corinthians 1:20

This is why in my last book, *Your Financial Revolution: The Power of Provision,* I told you that the Lord's Prayer is in the format of a legal requisition or petition. It is not asking when it says, "*Give us this day our daily bread.*" This is not a question; it is a requisition.

Just as my kids do not have to beg me for breakfast (they act like they own it with the, "Hey, Dad, pass the eggs."), so it is with the Kingdom—you already have a legal right to any and all of it through Jesus Christ.

Besides having legal access to what the Kingdom has in it, you are also a citizen of the Kingdom, which implies many more benefits, just as your citizenship in the United States has benefits that you would not otherwise be able to take advantage of.

> *Consequently, you are no longer foreigners and strangers, but fellow citizens with God's people and also members of his household.*
>
> —Ephesians 2:19

Finally, let's talk about that purse! Jesus said you need a purse, remember?

> *Sell your possessions and give to the poor. Provide purses for yourselves that will not wear out, a treasure in heaven that will never fail, where no thief comes near and no moth destroys. For where your treasure is, there your heart will be also.*
>
> —Luke 12:33-34

Provide purses for yourselves, a treasure in heaven that will never fail and where no one can take it from you. Let's get one thing cleared up right up front: Jesus is not saying that you must sell everything you own and just stay broke until you go to heaven. Remember, Paul is the same person who wrote 2 Corinthians 9 where he said that we would be made rich in every way so that we can be generous on every occasion. So, know that Paul is not implying that having money or having things is a sin and is wrong. Jesus is saying if money and things *have you*, then it would be better to sell them and realign your heart to a treasure that you cannot lose and that is eternal.

We grew up making money an idol. Money helps provide what we need in life; however, as so many have found out, money makes a miserable god. This is why Paul told Timothy to warn people who are wealthy to give and to be generous so they stay spiritually healthy. It is so easy for the heart to view money as an idol. Being generous is the antidote for greed. Practice it often.

> *Command those who are rich in this present world not to be arrogant nor to put their hope in wealth, which is so uncertain, but to put their hope in God, who richly provides us with everything for our enjoyment. Command them to do good, to be rich in good deeds, and to be generous and willing to share. In this way they will lay up treasure for themselves as a firm foundation for the coming age, so that they may take hold of the life that is truly life.*
>
> —1 Timothy 6:17-19

Notice that Paul tells Timothy to *command*, not *suggest*, those who are rich to be generous and to be willing to share. Remember, money is needed, but it is not life.

So where is your treasure?

Giving not only softens your heart toward God and people, but also it loosens the grip money has on your heart. The heart tends to envy and worship whatever you put in front of it, so we cannot let our hearts wander aimlessly. We must keep our hearts trained on God as our source. Giving confronts the greed that so easily tugs at our hearts.

So why do we have to give at all? Why can't God just help us financially without our giving? That is a good question, and we find the answer in Luke chapter 4.

First, God has no money, as I have stated previously. Secondly, He gave Adam complete and total dominion over the earth, as stated in Hebrews 2:7-8.

> *The devil led him up to a high place and showed him in an instant all the kingdoms of the world. And he said to him, "I will give you all their authority and splendor; it has been given to me, and I can give it to anyone I want to. If you worship me, it will all be yours."*
>
> *Jesus answered, "It is written: 'Worship the Lord your God and serve him only.'"*
>
> —Luke 4:5-8

This bit of Scripture is taking place when Satan is tempting Jesus in the wilderness. Satan tells Jesus that all the authority and splendor of the nations of the world have been given to him. And, yes, this is true. Adam had that position, but he gave it over to Satan when he committed treason against the Kingdom of God.

The splendor of a nation is its wealth, and the ability to rule over the wealth of nations was now ruled over by Satan. Don't get confused—the text does not say Satan gained *authority* over the splendor of the earth itself. God owns the earth and the fullness thereof. But the text does say that Satan has a *legal claim* on the wealth of the nations.

If you look at a piece of money, it is always minted or printed by a nation that has complete authority over its own currency. Because of what Adam did, God cannot legally make a claim on the currency of a nation or counterfeit it. However, if God can find someone in the earth realm who believes Him and is willing to sow money into His jurisdiction and authority, then God gains legal access and can step into that situation.

However, again, God has no money, so what do I mean when I say He can get involved with our finances? Although God cannot just make money appear like magic (that would be illegal because of Satan's legal claim), He can help you capture or create wealth.

OUR GIVING TO GOD OPENS THE DOOR OF RECIPROCITY, A VERY IMPORTANT LAW IN THE KINGDOM. WE REAP WHAT WE SOW.

Just like the stories I have referenced earlier in this book, generosity gives heaven legal jurisdiction to download instruction and direction to someone in the area of finances when they give. Remember the story of the fish in Luke chapter 5? Peter's willingness to loan Jesus the business's boat to preach from opened the legal door for the Holy Spirit to point out the fish that were available in the deep water.

Our giving to God opens the door of reciprocity, a very important law in the Kingdom. We reap what we sow.

So to make a long story short, we provide purses for ourselves by giving into the Kingdom and the work of God. Our giving gives us access to heaven's riches, which is why Paul called "giving" our purse. This changes everything in our lives. We are no longer limited by our own understanding. God, Himself is now helping us prosper.

> *You will be made rich in every way so that you can be generous in every way, which produces thanksgiving to God through us.*
>
> —2 Corinthians 9:11 (EHV)

Notice the Bible says you will *be made* rich, not that you must *strive to become* rich in your own strength and wisdom. No, you have a new partner—the Holy Spirit—and He knows a lot more than you do.

I can remember when we were broke for those nine stress-filled years. Money, or I should say the fear of not having enough money, had a strong grip on my heart. Even though I was a Christian, I had not developed my trust in God enough for my heart to change its allegiance from the broken earth curse system. I was trusting in the wrong treasure! At that point, my confidence was in *me*, and that was a poor choice to be sure.

God had to teach me how to provide a purse for myself to access His grace and ability. And although I think everyone who knows me knows how God did that, I want to relay the story again here in case you do not know how God did that. You know, God is pretty strategic; He knows exactly how to reach each of us.

I love to deer hunt but came up empty-handed for years. I would go out, sit in the cold, and go day after day with no luck. It was not that I just loved hunting; I had babies to feed and sure could have used the venison. Although I had some success in the past, it had been years since I had a successful deer season and brought home the meat.

One day, as I was thinking about the upcoming deer season, I heard the Lord's voice. He said, "Why don't you let Me show you how to get your deer this year?"

That startled me. *"Show me how to get my deer that year?"* What does that mean? Praying about those words, I felt impressed to sow a financial seed, or gift, for the exact purpose of harvesting that deer. I felt the Lord say to me that, when I sowed for my deer, I was to believe that I had already received it, before I actually got it, according to Mark 11:24.

> *Therefore, I tell you, whatever you ask for in prayer, believe that you have received it, and it will be yours.*
>
> —Mark 11:24

Although as a Christian, I had always given and supported my church, sowing like this, with a focused intent and believing that I receive when I pray, was new.

I took a check and wrote in the memo section, "For my 1987 deer." I laid my hands on it and declared that I just received my deer as I mailed it to a ministry I had confidence in.

Living in the Tulsa, Oklahoma, city limits at the time, I really did not have a place to hunt, but a friend of mine from church invited me to come down to his grandma's home in the country for Thanksgiving, and he said there were a few deer around the farm. So, my family headed down Thanksgiving morning to enjoy a great day of food and fellowship, and to bag my deer.

My friend did not really know where to tell me to go, but there was a pasture that was bordered by woods, and he suggested that I go out to the pasture and sit next to a big tree that was there.

Now, I want you to get this picture. I was sitting in a mowed hay pasture that had one big tree in the middle. Looking back on it, I was just sitting out there in the open field next to a tree. As it got light, I thought, *This will never work sitting out in the open. I need to find a better place to sit.*

As I was thinking about getting up and moving toward the woods, I was unaware of what was happening behind me on the other side of that tree. Without me knowing it, a buck was running across the field behind me. The tree was between the deer and me, so the buck did not see me, and I did not see it. The buck ran to the tree, caught my scent, and came to a sudden stop as it tried to figure out what was going on.

As the buck stopped and looked around the tree, we made eye contact. The buck was only five yards away! The buck wasted no time shifting into high gear. With a loud snort, it took off at full speed.

Now, I will have to admit that I am not a great shot. Trying to line up on a whitetail buck that was running at full speed directly away from me did not offer me a large target. Secondly, pulling off an offhand shot with a scoped out 30-06 was not the easiest shot to take. But when I pulled the trigger, the buck fell and did not move. I was shocked! At the sound of the rifle, my friend came out and congratulated me on my buck, as he saw it laying there. I had not told my friend about what the Lord had told me, but I looked at him and said, "I don't think this deer was due to my great hunting ability."

I pulled the piece of paper that I had written on the day I mailed that check out of my hunting coat. It simply said, "I believe that I receive my 1987 deer, in the name of Jesus." I had the date and time I prayed written there as well. I held up the paper for my friend to see and then began telling him about what the Lord told me to do.

This event caught my attention. I know without a doubt getting that buck was a God thing. Of course, when you see something like that, your mind tries to suggest that it was just a fluke. But for the last 34 years, I have harvested my deer using the same method as I did for that 1987 deer, without fail, usually in just under an hour in the woods.

God used the same method to reach Peter, James, and John that day on the Lake of Gennesaret. The Bible says they were astonished at what they saw.

> *For he and all his companions were astonished at the catch of fish they had taken, and so were James and John, the sons of Zebedee, Simon's partners.*
> *Then Jesus said to Simon, "Don't be afraid; from now on you will fish for people." So they pulled their boats up on shore, left everything and followed him.*
> —Luke 5:9-11

They were so astonished that they left everything and followed Jesus. They saw a better way of doing things, a much better way.

As God showed me the Kingdom and how to provide the purse (access point to my treasure in heaven) that I needed, my heart grew more confidence in my heavenly resources than what I held in my hand.

God taught me that I could sow for anything I needed, and He would either give me a plan to create the money or a plan to capture it.

I do not have space here to share all of the amazing things I have seen as a result of the Kingdom, but I can say that Drenda and I have seen some pretty incredible things happen financially. From being totally and absolutely broke to being financially free and able to support ministry by the millions over the years is an amazing thing.

Sowing in faith for a specific harvest was one of the first things God taught me as I began to learn of the Kingdom. Although I do not have time in this book to cover everything, in my other books, you will find the stories of how specific the Kingdom is and how specific your seed needs to be. My *Your Financial Revolution: The Power of Provision* book covers the steps to release your faith and how to specifically sow your seed more than this book does. I encourage you to get a copy and learn more about this topic.

This book covers some key Kingdom principles that God taught me about being generous and giving. I hope they encourage you and inspire you to want to learn more and be all that God has for you.

CHAPTER 9
THE LAW OF THE MEASURE

Several months ago, Drenda and I sowed $15,000 into another ministry. As I was about to release my faith, the Holy Spirit reminded me of 2 Corinthians 9:10-11, and I couldn't get that Scripture out of my head for a few days after that.

> *Now he who supplies seed to the sower and bread for food will also supply and increase your store of seed and will enlarge the harvest of your righteousness. You will be enriched in every way so that you can be generous on every occasion, and through us your generosity will result in thanksgiving to God.*
>
> —2 Corinthians 9:10-11

I was meditating on the part where it says God gives seed to the sower and bread for food, and "bread for food" jumped out at me. I realized that so many people face fear when they want to give because they do not understand that phrase. Most people think that when they give, they are giving up something, that it is going to *cost* them. But what God was reminding me of was that not only does He provide the seed to sow, but He also provides the bread for eating, or what a person needs personally. Of course, I already knew that, but

I felt that He wanted to make sure I told people that—that He gives us both, and we do not need to be afraid to give.

On this particular night, a couple of weeks after we had sown the $15,000, I was about to turn the lights off and head to bed when, suddenly, I had a thought to check on a few stocks I own to see how they were doing in the market. As I pulled up my account, I saw that they had indeed moved up some.

I was about to put my phone down when my eyes were drawn to one particular stock that I did not own. I had seen this stock before, and I had looked at it once to consider buying it. When I investigated its past performance, I saw that it was flat for the last 12 months, so I passed.

But for some reason, this night, this stock seemed to jump out to me. Strangely, I felt that I should buy some of it, which was totally out of character for me. So, I went ahead and bought $1,500 of this stock and set my phone down.

Drenda and I talked for a little bit, and I told her about the stock purchase. Then, I pulled it up to show her. When I pulled it up, I was shocked. It had gone up over 100 percent in only an hour! We stayed awake and talked as we watched the numbers slowly keep going up.

Over the next three hours, the stock had moved up to being worth over $17,000, where it leveled off. I told Drenda, "That is our $15,000!"

I quickly sold the stock and captured the increase. The stock went back down by the next morning and has never regained that level of increase now months after that event occurred. It was the weirdest thing I have ever seen. I know that it was the Holy Spirit who illuminated that stock to me, and I told Drenda it was God returning our seed. God gives seed to the sower, and He gives bread for the eating! You know, I don't care how He does it, but He always does it!

But it was interesting. After I sold that stock and had the money back in my account, I thought, *Boy, if I knew it was going to go up like that, I would have put a lot more than $1,500 in.* Looking back is always 20/20 vision. Yes, I could have put $10,000 in, or your mind drifts and thinks, *What if I had put $100,000 in? Think of the amount of money I would have made on that investment.* But I didn't put $100,000 in. I didn't put $10,000 in. I didn't even put $5,000 in; I put $1,500 in. My profit was capped. I put in $1,500, and although I sure would have liked more, that was not going to happen because I only put in $1,500.

The Bible tells us in Luke 6:38 what happened, why I did not make more money that night.

> *Give, and it will be given to you. A good measure, pressed down, shaken together and running over, will be poured into your lap. For with the measure you use, it will be measured to you."*
>
> —Luke 6:38

See, I set the measure, and it was measured back to me by my own measure—the potential I had that night was directly proportionate to what I put in. I set the measure, and with that same measure, I reaped a return. Jesus says this same principle applies to your giving as well.

There is a story in the Bible that I want to show you where this happened. We can learn a lot more about the law of the measure from it.

> *The wife of a man from the company of the prophets cried out to Elisha, "Your servant my husband is dead, and you know*

that he revered the Lord. But now his creditor is coming to take my two boys as his slaves."

Elisha replied to her, "How can I help you? Tell me, what do you have in your house?"

"Your servant has nothing there at all," she said, "except a small jar of olive oil."

Elisha said, "Go around and ask all your neighbors for empty jars. Don't ask for just a few. Then go inside and shut the door behind you and your sons. Pour oil into all the jars, and as each is filled, put it to one side."

She left him and shut the door behind her and her sons. They brought the jars to her and she kept pouring. When all the jars were full, she said to her son, "Bring me another one."

But he replied, "There is not a jar left." Then the oil stopped flowing.

She went and told the man of God, and he said, "Go, sell the oil and pay your debts. You and your sons can live on what is left."

—2 Kings 4:1-7

This is a great story with so much Kingdom revelation in it.

This woman goes to the prophet for help. She is in debt and about to lose her sons. But interestingly enough, the prophet does not pull money out of his treasury. Instead, he asks her a very strange question in light of the circumstances: "What do you have in your house?"

I think the question took the woman by surprise, as you can almost hear her surprise in how she answers. "I have nothing at all!" she said. She adds the "at all" for emphasis. But she does mention what she does have. It's not much, but she has a small amount of olive oil. That is all the prophet needed to hear. That was the answer. Look carefully at his instructions.

Elisha said, "Go around and ask all your neighbors for empty jars. <u>Don't ask for just a few.</u>

Don't ask for a few. How many is that? I think you would agree that the number of jars she should have gathered is open for debate as only she could define what that meant to her. She was about to find out that she had definitely not gathered enough jars!

She left him and shut the door behind her and her sons. They brought the jars to her and she kept pouring. When all the jars were full, she said to her son, "Bring me another one."

But he replied, "There is not a jar left." Then the oil stopped flowing.

Note when the oil stopped flowing—not at a specified number of jars but when she ran out of jars. When all the jars were full, she told her son to bring her another one, and he said there was not a jar left. I'm sure she would have liked it to continue, but she only gathered so many jars. Her increase was capped not by God but by her own thinking.

I am sure she probably wished she would have had more jars, many more jars. And if she really understood what was about to happen, I am sure she would have knocked on every door in town looking for jars. She might have even sent requests out to other cities to gather jars.

The story had a good outcome though: her debts were paid, and the family lived on what was left after they sold the oil.

But what could the outcome have been? She could have paid off the debt of *everyone* that she knew, built a new town square, and helped so many people.

So why did she only gather the number of jars that she did? I believe the answer is she had a survival mentality. She was focused on the pressure point—the amount she was in debt for and what she thought it would take to continue to raise her sons. Instead of thinking past the pressure, she was focused on just eliminating it. I believe if she had gathered a thousand jars, they would have all been filled. She set the measure!

God gives all of us the same opportunity that the woman had. We all must choose how we want to set the measure.

Let me explain as we review our key Scripture for this chapter.

> *Give, and it will be given to you. A good measure, pressed down, shaken together and running over, will be poured into your lap. For with the measure you use, it will be measured to you.*
>
> —Luke 6:38

We all love to quote the first part of this Scripture—that if we give, we will reap with running over abundance. But many times, we fail to read the last part, the part that says we will only reap *according to the same measure that we used in giving.*

Why is this principle so vital to you and me? Well, let me give an example.

Let's say you are a beginning farmer and I told you that I wanted to purchase 5,000 bushels of wheat. You and I agree on a price per bushel, and you prepare to plant your 10-acre field with wheat for the harvest.

I think you know what will happen. You will fall terribly short in the bushels needed to fulfill our contract. Why? Because you have no idea how many acres it takes to harvest 5,000 bushels of wheat.

HOW MANY CHRISTIANS ARE LINING TRUCKS UP PREPARING TO TAKE THEIR HARVESTS TO MARKET BUT HAVE ONLY PLANTED TWO TOMATO PLANTS?

The measure in the farmer's example is the number of acres he planted. In the woman's case, it was the number of jars she gathered. In Jesus's example, it is the amount that we sow.

So, if the harvest we are expecting is not possible with the measure we set to receive it, then we have disappointment, and possibly people of little understanding could even blame God for what appears as a failure of His Word.

So here is the million-dollar question: If a farmer needs 5,000 bushels of wheat and has no clue how many acres he needs to plant, what should he do?

Ask a farmer who knows!

Now let's put this principle into a real-life situation that I see all the time.

A family wants to pay off a $300,000 mortgage, and they know they need to sow and come into agreement as husband and wife and release their faith. But how much should they sow? I get this question all the time. How much do they need to sow to set the measure for a $300,000 harvest? They have no idea. They would need to ask someone who knows, and that would be the Holy Spirit.

We have all heard Him whisper the answer to that question many times. Usually without good teaching, we simply dismiss that small voice as something we cannot do. For instance, as you are sowing for XYZ, you sense that you should sow $1,000. Immediately, your mind steps in and says, "No, I can't do that," or even worse, "Satan, get behind me."

One thing you can be sure of is that <u>Satan will never tell you to sow more into the Kingdom</u>. He is fully aware of this law of the Kingdom. So, in this case, because you have not developed confidence in the principle of setting the measure, when your mind argues, you give in and give your usual $100. And, of course, like my wheat example, you fall terribly short of your needed harvest.

Now, before I go any further, I do need to clarify one thing:

The amount you give is not simply dictated by the amount of money you are sowing!

Look at Luke 21:1-4:

> *As Jesus looked up, he saw the rich putting their gifts into the temple treasury. He also saw a poor widow put in two very small copper coins. "Truly I tell you," he said, "this poor widow has put in more than all the others. All these people gave their gifts out of their wealth; but she out of her poverty put in all she had to live on."*

Notice that Jesus said the poor widow gave more than all the wealthy people who gave that day. The wealthy gave a lot more money, but the Bible says they gave it out of their wealth, or we can say out of their extra money. The poor widow gave out of her very life, and it took great faith.

It does not take faith to give out of your extra. Of course, giving generously out of your overflow is a good thing to do, but in that day, people could watch what people were putting in, and the wealthy, many times, gave to be seen by men and to gain a religious stature among their peers.

So an equation of simply setting the measure by the amount of money you give is not an accurate definition of how we set the measure. It is a very big part but is not the only part.

We need to remember that what is "big" to one person is not necessarily big to another.

In the early days, giving a thousand dollars was a HUGE amount of money for me. In fact, when we started, we would have to pay that offering out over a few months. But our ability grew, and we have been able to give much more as our faith and confidence have grown.

Here is what I tell people: When you sow for provision, take a moment and ask the Holy Spirit what to sow and where to sow it.

Usually, sowing for routine needs does not take as much faith as sowing for a major breakthrough, such as your home being paid off, would take. When I sow for major things, I always want to *feel* it. What I mean is that I do not just want to give out of my extra money. I want to sow enough that I can *feel* my faith engage. The amount must be big enough that it might prompt my flesh to react and I hear in my mind, *Are you sure about this?*

I have found that the Holy Spirit will tell you the amount when you ask Him; just be sure you really want to hear Him.

I have had to have help here many times. Because I pay the bills, it is always easier for Drenda to hear the amount we should sow and not have any hesitation. Do you remember the story I told you about sowing that $200,000 into our Faith Life campus for the first time?

Well, I did not tell you all of the details of that story. This was to be a three-year commitment, not a debt but a goal that we set to give over that period of time. When the day came that we were to make our intentions known and sow our initial seed, I really thought

$150,000 was all that I wanted to give. But Drenda argued with me that she heard we were to give $200,000. I dismissed her input and held my ground at $150,000. In the actual service, again she insisted that we give $200,000, but again I refused.

Right before we were to sow our seed that day, a farmer in my church stood up and asked to speak. He encouraged everyone there to trust God for their harvests. He went on to explain that, as a farmer, he was dependent on the laws of sowing and reaping to survive and had found them to be trustworthy. He said he spends $200,000 every year just to plant his seed. Then he went on to say that, at first, it might look foolish to just throw $200,000 into the dirt because once sown, there would be no way to recapture it. But he emphasized the law of sowing and reaping always prevails with a harvest that is much bigger than the $200,000 he spends sowing his fields.

Drenda gave me a light jab in the side. I took the hint—$200,000 it was, and that is what we sowed. And you remember how God moved on that vice president to give us the yearly bonus that year—the exact amount of $200,000. It did not cost us a penny to sow that seed. And, as I said in that earlier chapter, that bonus has been in place for years now and has paid us well over $2 million of income.

See, Drenda's mind was not full of the details of all the bills, leaving no room for fear to try to rise up. She simply heard God. And in reality, that is all I needed to do as well. But this was the first time we sowed anything close to that amount, so yes, I was giving in to fear when I held to $150,000. I thank God for my wife, who encouraged me to trust the Lord for that higher amount

It will *always* take faith to sow, *always*. So let's not allow fear to stop us from harvesting all that God is trying to get to us.

Remember this: Whoever sows sparingly will also reap

sparingly, and whoever sows generously will also reap generously.
—2 Corinthians 9:6

In this text, Paul is collecting an offering for another church, and he is reminding the people of a principle that he apparently had taught to them before, that they will reap what they sow and according to the measure they sow. Paul is stating the principle of setting the measure.

When Peter gave his boat to Jesus to use that day on the lake, we saw that James and John's boat filled up to the exact harvest that Peter's faith had brought in because they were partners. But let me ask you this: If Peter had 1,000 boats that day in his business, how many boats would have filled up?

If you said 1,000, you're correct.

Again, we see the measure being set. The measure given is the *container* that God can fill. So, I encourage you to set the measure with a big vision. You do not want to look back and say, "Wow, that stock went up a thousand percent in three hours. I wish I would have put in more."

So, what prompted me to put in only $1,500 that night after being prompted by the Holy Spirit to buy? Well, for me, it was that I just did not ask God to tell me the amount. I was just acting from my own mind, and I missed His voice.

Now, please do not go out and buy a bunch of stocks because of this story. As I said earlier, I do not put much money in the stock market. But God made His point that night—He gives seed for sowing and bread for eating, and it was a good reminder that *we* set the measure.

I hope you remember this story the next time God taps you on the shoulder to fund an assignment.

We all have to allow God to train us in this.

I can remember when Florida property values fell during the 2009 crash. We had friends there that lived on the coast, and we would visit them often. During that time, there were houses for sale all over Florida. As we were walking down the beach with our friend one day, he said, "I want to show you something."

We walked up to a house that had a for sale sign on it. The price was only $695,000 for the two houses on the property. (Yes, you read that right, two houses on the beach for $695,000. They would come furnished as well. I think we would both agree that was a steal.) One was rented out and would produce great income, as these houses were right on the beach. But I just could not see spending that kind of money at that moment in time, and I passed on buying them. (I know, I know, not too smart.) My friend had multiple houses already and did not want the job of managing two more at the time. I mean, he walked us right up to them. It is not every day that a multimillionaire would take you into his counsel and say, "Here is what I would do." Of course, Drenda was saying we should buy, but I did not budge.

Well, you can guess the outcome. Those two houses were sold and resold a few years later for $3 million.

SO, DO NOT LET FEAR SPEAK TO YOU WHEN YOU ARE SOWING AND SETTING YOUR MEASURE. BE BOLD.

You know what the saddest and most disappointing thing was? I did not even pray about it that day. I put aside the wisdom of the Holy Spirit. I ignored the wisdom of my friend and my wife, who is very wise. I still said no because I knew it would have taken all of our available cash at the time, and with the economy blowing up, I just didn't feel comfortable doing it. But as I said, I did not ask

God about it, which was a costly mistake.

Unfortunately, I have missed many harvests (not all but many), and God has had to deal with me about it.

One day years ago, Drenda just so happened to run into Kenneth Copeland while she was at a resort, and he invited her to have breakfast with him and his wife, Gloria.

At the table, Kenneth said he had a word for Drenda and me. She recorded it on her phone for me as I was not with her on that trip. It went something like this:

> "I have tried to bring you houses and lands, but you would not let Me."

Wow, that was a rebuke. But as I thought back on so many things I had said no to, I saw my error. So, I made up my mind that from that day on, I was not going to miss my harvest ever again. Once I made that decision, it was amazing how fast God brought those things to me that I had sown for.

So, do not let fear speak to you when you are sowing and setting your measure. Be bold. You will not know how God is going to bring these things to pass, just as I am sure the widow in 2 Kings 4 could not have imagined that the oil would just keep flowing. If she had, her story would have been a completely different story. We would probably still be reading about the poor widow who became a billionaire in the oil business today.

Finally, remember you will always be sowing into a greater and greater harvest. You are living today from yesterday's harvest, so you want to keep that in mind when you are sowing.

Also, remember that it is always the darkest just after you sow. The seed bin looks empty and the plants have not yet begun to sprout. But you hold to the Word of God, stand strong, and pray in the Spirit for the direction and details of the harvest that God is bringing to you.

I want to end this chapter with a story I have told many times but that bears repeating. It involves one of my salesmen, years ago, when I was first learning the principle of setting the measure. He was building a new home and, as most new home builds tend to do, they went over budget. Something is always changed or added that changes the final price.

Well, in this case, my friend had already exhausted all of the money that the bank had allocated, and he came up short. If I remember the issue, he did not have all the money to pay for the kitchen cabinets. I think he was somewhere around $25,000 short.

One night, one of my other reps went along with the rep who was building the house to a worship service. Toward the end of the message, the preacher was taking up an offering for a certain cause, and I did not get the details on it, but the sales rep who went with the rep who was building his house came to me and said that the sales rep who was building his house seemed to be struggling with something that night.

He explained that this guy who was building his house walked up to the front of the church and gave his offering and then came back and took his seat. But he seemed agitated. He then told me that he got up and went back down to the front and gave more money. Coming back to his seat, he seemed even more agitated that time. He sat there for a few minutes, and then, with a groan, he went up front again and gave more money. That time when he came back, he seemed at peace and the agitation was gone.

Later that month, the rep who was building his house gave the testimony that he was sowing that night at church for the money he needed to get those kitchen cabinets paid for. If I remember correctly, the builder decided to discount the cabinets by 50%, and he was able to close enough business to get the final bill paid.

So, what was happening that night? The rep who was building his house told me that he just did not have peace until the third time he went up and gave all that he had. See, he had been praying about how to pay that $25,000, and the Holy Spirit was leading him to set the measure needed to bring in the harvest he was looking for.

So, remember this very important law of the Kingdom, the law of the measure, the next time you are sowing.

CHAPTER 10
THE GENEROUS KING

I am sure we have all done this. Someone walks up and gives us a compliment, and we say something like, "Oh, I bought this at a garage sale for $5."

Why do we say something like that? Why do we feel shame for having something nice? It is interesting and sad that when we built our new home out in the country over 20 years ago, we actually prayed that it would be big on the inside but look small on the outside. We were new pastors, and we felt that people would get upset if we were building a big house. At the time, we were not taking any income from the church—it was money from our own business that we were using to build—but for some reason, we felt people would think we were taking it from the church. So we built a home with 7,700 square feet of space, but if you look at the house, it looks basically like a normal two story house.

Later, we realized how dumb that was. Why should we be ashamed of the blessing of the Lord?

I use this analogy in my conferences.

Suppose I crawled onto the platform wearing ragged and dirty clothes and declared that today is a celebration; today Drenda and I paid our house off. Then I shared how hard we had worked (sometimes 80 hours a week) to get it done, but we did it.

Everyone would clap and shout. Why? Because someone actually beat the system. There is a way out.

But if I walked up to the platform and said, "Today, a stranger walked up and handed us $1 million, and we have paid our house off."

Everyone would say that was not fair. Why? Because we have been raised in the earth curse system of painful toil and sweat. That is how we have been trained to acquire provision. Of course, it is a system of slavery, as most never enjoy any sense of real financial freedom. And because of this, most never discover their real purpose, their spiritual DNA. Because of the survival system we live under, most financial decisions are made around *money*, not *purpose*. People dream of being free to pursue their dreams and passions, but for most, that never happens.

A few years ago, God began to deal with me about the double portion and how it is ours. The double portion sets us free from the earth curse system of survival and leaning to painful toil and sweat just to survive.

In a nutshell, the double portion means *more than enough*. Having more than enough allows us to live debt free and to be on assignment instead of selling our lives for money.

Although I had talked about the double portion in my conferences for years, I felt that the Lord wanted to show me something about it that I had not yet understood. I knew there was more than I was seeing, and I asked the Holy Spirit to show me what it was.

I began to study the Scriptures that pertained to the double portion and waited for the Lord to show me what I was missing. Well, He caught my attention with the most dramatic demonstration of what He was trying to get across to me that I could have ever imagined.

I received a call from a gentleman that I had never met, one of our ministry partners. After reading my books, he understood that I loved to hunt, so he called and said, "I want to buy you a shotgun. What kind do you not have?"

At the time, I had the usual all-around basic shotgun that I used for everything from deer hunting to hunting ducks, pheasants, and rabbits. I also had a 20 gauge double side-by-side that my father bought me when I was 16. But I had always been intrigued by the beautiful over and under shotguns I had seen many times in the hunting magazines. They always had beautiful engraving and perfect wooden stocks and were always finished to perfection. So, I told him that I did not have an over and under and really had always wanted one. I was in shock when he said that he was going to send me one. That was unusual for sure, and I was thrilled.

Sure enough, a week later, a box came to my church office, and when I opened it, there was not one but *two* of the most beautiful over and under shotguns that I had ever seen.

I quickly called my partner and thanked him for such an awesome gift.

The next week, he sent me two more! I now had four of the best guns I have ever owned. I called him again, and he said that so often, people never call and thank him for his gifts; and because I had done so, he thought he just might send me two more. Obviously, I knew this was something God was up to. I mean they were coming two at a time, and I had been asking Him about the double portion.

Well, to make a long story short, guns began to come in the mail, always in pairs. Before long, I had probably FOURTEEN new shotguns, all of the highest quality. These were not cheap guns. These guns were worth thousands of dollars.

Then, I had two pearl white Cadillac Escalade SUVs given to me.

At the time, we were driving our ten-year-old Honda Pilot, which we loved (Hondas are always great cars), but they are not Escalades.

Drenda had wanted a Louis Vuitton purse for a few years, and I gave her one as a special Christmas present a couple of years ago. But on her birthday this year, she received—you guessed it—TWO Louis Vuitton purses, each from different people.

We also had our second airplane show up in this season, as well as two ocean beach houses show up, and to top it all off, at Christmas, two black mink coats were given to us, each worth $10,000.

Let me pause and emphasize that I am not trying to brag here, because I did not do any of it!!!! The guns just showed up. The two white Escalades just showed up. The purses just showed up. The mink coats just showed up.

The two houses, of course, were more involved, but we had sown seed for a beach house a few years earlier. I did not know it, and she did not tell me at the time, but a few years earlier, Drenda had found a house she loved in a real estate magazine. She remembers pointing to the picture and saying, "Lord, I want that one." At the time, we had too many other financial commitments and projects to actually have the cash available to pull the trigger on a Florida home, but we knew one would show up at the right season.

One day as I was jogging, the Lord spoke to me and said, "*Send Drenda to Florida tomorrow to buy her Florida home.*" There was a certain urgency with the tomorrow part, so I said, "Wow. Well, okay, Lord."

So, Drenda went down to Florida and looked at 25 different houses. Among the houses she looked at, one kept drawing her back toward it as being the house for her.

I flew down and looked at it with her and agreed that it was perfect. (All of this time, she had forgotten about the day she pointed to that real estate magazine and declared that she would own that house. It had been about three years at that point, and we had never seen the house that she had pointed to in person.)

We put a contract on the house that she wanted; and one day, while we were sitting in our home in Ohio working through some of the contract required inspection reports, Drenda suddenly yelled out, "That's my house!"

I was taken aback, as we were in contract and everything was a go for closing. "Of course it is your house," I said.

"You do not understand," she said. "That is the *exact house* that I pointed to in the real estate magazine a few years ago!"

Then I remembered that the real estate magazine she was looking at three years ago featured homes in the same town. Could it be the same house? Drenda was sure it was the same house, and she began to name the features of the home that had caught her attention years earlier. They matched this home exactly. So I did some research, and sure enough, the house we were buying was indeed listed for sale the year and the time of year that Drenda said she pointed to it and declared that she would own it. But then I saw that, for some reason, basically right after she had declared that she would own it, it was taken off the market.

As I studied the history of this house, I realized that it had been off the market all this time until just a few days earlier when it went back on the market. No wonder the Holy Spirit said to send her down to Florida tomorrow!

So, we purchased that beach house, and Drenda finally had her house, something she had dreamed of her entire life. Then we inherited a second beach home in Canada in that same year. Wow!

If you have not noticed, everything that God sent to us was top end stuff; I mean top end. We were in a bit of shock over all that had happened. But the Lord spoke to me and said, *"I know you do not NEED fourteen shotguns. I know that you do not need two white Escalades..."* and He went through the whole list.

Then He said, *"I do not want My children to be need conscious. They own the whole estate, and it is My good pleasure to give My children good things."*

HE REMINDED ME THAT HE IS THE GOD OF MORE THAN ENOUGH, THE GOD OF THE DOUBLE PORTION.

He reminded me that He is the God of more than enough, the God of the double portion. He then went on to say that His people are not thinking big enough, not dreaming big enough, and they are limiting what He could do for them.

Drenda and I were a little taken aback by all that the Lord was showing us. We realized that we needed to tell people about the double portion. The double portion does not literally mean two of everything—the Lord was using that to catch my attention. The double portion means *more than enough.*

God then told me that I was to teach this to my church, and I was to tell them of everything that He sent to us and how it came about.

Now, Drenda and I are pretty private about what we have, because things are not life, and we certainly never want to place an emphasis on having things or making things what you seek. But we did not seek these things; God sent them. So, we taught the double portion over an 11-week period at church, and I think it had probably the most profound effect on our people's finances than any other series I have ever taught.

But you know what? I also had people leave the church because they were offended by what I shared. They thought I did not need all of those guns, or two Escalades, or two beach houses, or two airplanes, or two beautiful fur coats. They thought that I was just bragging and making a big deal over *stuff*.

But they missed the whole point—God was showing us that He is more than enough. His Kingdom is not cloaked in survival like the earth realm is. His Kingdom is a kingdom of more than enough, and He delights in taking great care of His children.

I had to remind people that I did not do this. God did it to make a point—not that everyone should be driving an expensive car but because He wants us to stop settling and limiting Him. He wants us to stop saying no out of habit, limiting Him from what He wants to do. He wants us to know that He is the God of more than enough.

This understanding is so important in our discussion of being generous. You have to have something to be generous with, especially to be able to be generous on *every* occasion. I know He had my attention, and I learned to never be ashamed of the goodness of God.

The next fall, a local pastor asked if he could hunt on my land. I always tell folks that I do not allow any hunting until my kids and I all have our deer, then I will allow a few people in before the season closes. Well, that fall we all had our deer in the freezer, so I invited this pastor to come over.

The day he came over, I met him outside to give him some direction as to where he should hunt. I saw that he was using an old bird gun, meaning it just had a brass bead on it to aim with. It was not designed to hunt deer. You have to be close to the deer, because the old bird guns were not designed to be accurate with a deer slug. But, of course, you can use them, as I did a few times over my hunting career.

But as I sat there talking to him, I remembered that one of the guns God sent me was a really nice deer hunting shotgun. In fact, it was top of the line. I felt the Holy Spirit say, *"Why don't you give this pastor that deer hunting shotgun that was given to you? You have a few other deer hunting guns, but he does not have a good gun to hunt with."*

So, I gave him that shotgun, and he was so happy. That gift spoke to him of God's goodness and encouraged him toward God.

Remember what I told you a few chapters ago—that some of the money and some of the stuff you are holding is not for you? God sent it to you to meet someone else's need.

I said all that to say this: You abide in a generous Kingdom with a generous King, but you will never enjoy all the Kingdom has in it if you do not break that poverty spirit driving you to hoard everything you ever get.

I know you have probably watched the TV show about hoarders where they actually do an intervention. The home is so crammed full of junk you cannot even walk through it. In many cases, the home has to be torn down or rebuilt because it is in such disrepair. This is how our hearts look when we are full of greed and want to just hoard everything for a rainy day. Money and possessions need to be held lightly.

It is really hard to be generous when you are consumed with survival. God wants you to know that there is plenty in His house, so feel free to be generous. Your generosity invites people into the Kingdom of God and opens their hearts to receive His goodness and generosity. Remember, it is the goodness of God that leads people to repentance.

> *For the kingdom of heaven is like a landowner who went out early in the morning to hire workers for his vineyard. He agreed to pay them a denarius for the day and sent them into his vineyard.*

About nine in the morning he went out and saw others standing in the marketplace doing nothing. He told them, "You also go and work in my vineyard, and I will pay you whatever is right." So they went.

He went out again about noon and about three in the afternoon and did the same thing. About five in the afternoon he went out and found still others standing around. He asked them, "Why have you been standing here all day long doing nothing?"

"Because no one has hired us," they answered.

He said to them, "You also go and work in my vineyard."

When evening came, the owner of the vineyard said to his foreman, "Call the workers and pay them their wages, beginning with the last ones hired and going on to the first."

The workers who were hired about five in the afternoon came and each received a denarius. So when those came who were hired first, they expected to receive more. But each one of them also received a denarius. When they received it, they began to grumble against the landowner. "These who were hired last worked only one hour," they said, "and you have made them equal to us who have borne the burden of the work and the heat of the day."

But he answered one of them, "I am not being unfair to you, friend. Didn't you agree to work for a denarius? Take your pay and go. I want to give the one who was hired last the same as I gave you. Don't I have the right to do what I want with my own money? Or are you envious because I am generous?"

So the last will be first, and the first will be last.

—Matthew 20:1-16

In this parable, these workers missed the whole point! Instead of grumbling against the owner, they should have been thankful and so grateful for the opportunity to work for him. They should have considered that to find someone to work for who was that generous could offer them many opportunities down the road. I mean, do you want to work for a stingy boss or for someone who is extremely generous? If they had any common sense, they would have made arrangements on the spot to work there the next day, and the next day after that, and so on.

Unfortunately, this is just like church folk. When they see someone prospering in a big way, they think, *Well, that's not fair. I do not have that happening in my life.* For instance, when they see that God sent me all those shotguns, instead of thinking, *Wow! God did that for him* or *God did that for them; He can do the same thing for me!* they get offended and grumble at God and at me!

Friend, do you get envious of others at a Chinese buffet? (I love a Chinese buffet, but plug in whatever kind of buffet you want.) Do you ever get envious seeing a person going to their seat with a heaping plate of food at a buffet? Of course not. You have no reason to because you know there is plenty there for everyone.

In fact, if you were sitting there eating your one plate at the buffet, and you noticed that one person had gone up 10 times, would you be envious? Would you be angry with them? No again, because you knew that the price included all you wanted. But if you thought that there was a very limited supply of food, and you were a long way back in the line to get your first plate, and then you watched this guy go up 10 times, you might get angry and call it unfair. But that is not the Kingdom you live in, friend. We are all equal! God is generous to us all equally, so don't grumble. Just get in line!

One day, I received a letter from a lady who watched me on TV. She was upset that I had a Cadillac Escalade. I suppose she wanted me to drive a horse and buggy; I am not sure. But she went on about how teaching about money was so wrong. So, I called her.

I asked her why it was wrong to have money. Of course, she did not have a valid reason except that it was greed and God hates greed. I told her I agree that God hates greed as it is idolatry. Then, I asked her how much money she gave in the last year to reach the world with the Gospel. She was silent. I told her that Drenda and I personally paid for an entire crusade in Pakistan that year at which 100,000 people were saved. The lady did not have much to say after that.

FRIEND, WE ARE CALLED TO BE GENEROUS, AND GENEROSITY REQUIRES YOU TO HAVE SOMETHING TO GIVE.

Friend, we are called to be generous, and generosity requires you to have something to give. But if you have a "money is bad mindset" or believe a vow of poverty is righteous, then you will not be able to receive, and you will be stuck before you can even start.

CHAPTER 11
THE PROMISE TO THOSE WHO ARE GENEROUS

Bill and his wife, April, have owned a small family-run plumbing business for 14 years. As members of Faith Life Church, they have seen all the growth that has occurred over the years as well as all the stories of victory. So when they heard that we are going to expand Faith Life Church to have a greater community impact, they were totally on board.

April shared that she was fully prepared to give $10,000 toward the project, but she was totally surprised when Bill came home from the grocery store and told her the Lord had told him to give $75,000, not $10,000.

They had no idea how that would be possible, but April agreed to give $75,000 toward the expansion. But again, they did not have the money or any idea where that kind of money would come from.

A few weeks later, the city water department called and told them that they were doing a major repair project and asked if they would be interested in bidding on it. They said yes and began the legal steps and paperwork required to perform a city job. April said the contract was over 100 pages long, and they also had to get a bond in place. It was quite a process to get that all wrapped up, but they got it done. They found out they were the only company that submitted a bid on the project, and they had no idea how or why they were contacted to apply.

Once they submitted the contract, the city called them in and told them that they felt they were too small of a company to handle the job as they had to complete the work on 200 houses in just 75 days. But after some discussion, they convinced the city that they could handle it.

Bill says it was an all-hands-on-deck project with the team working late hours as well as Saturday hours. But you know what? They finished it on time and were able to generously give $75,000 to the church project as well as pay off all of their consumer debt in the process. They were thrilled!

See, God had a bigger plan for Bill and April than they had for themselves. He knew their hearts for Him, but He wanted to stretch them, stretch their capacity.

Now, having already been approved for government work and having finished a successful contract for the city, the door is open to even bigger contracts in the future.

God loves to stretch people. He knows our potential, but we often don't know our own potential and usually need a bit of nudging. This is a pattern that you need to get accustomed to.

> *Again, it will be like a man going on a journey, who called his servants and entrusted his wealth to them. To one he gave five bags of gold, to another two bags, and to another one bag, each according to his ability. Then he went on his journey. The man who had received five bags of gold went at once and put his money to work and gained five bags more. So also, the one with two bags of gold gained two more. But the man who had received one bag went off, dug a hole in the ground and hid his master's money.*
>
> —Matthew 25:14-18

We read this parable before, but I want to point out something that we have not looked at.

Notice that when the owner handed out the assignments to his servants, it says the assignments were handed out "each according to his ability." The one that was given five bags of gold was trusted with five bags, meaning he currently had the capacity to manage five bags. If he had a greater ability, or capacity, the owner would have given him more. The same goes for the other two servants.

But look at what happened. The servant with the five bags of gold increased it to ten bags. In that process, what has happened? Well, in simple terms, his ability, or capacity, increased from a level five to a level ten. His capacity to handle responsibility and management increased. He became much more valuable to the owner and postured himself for further promotion.

Now, here is the wisdom of the owner. He knew the character of the servant with the five bags of gold. He knew he had the potential to rise to that new level. Although the owner gave the servant five bags of gold, which was his current level of capacity, the assignment he gave the servant with those five bags of gold would harvest more than what the servant started out with and would push him to a new level of management capacity.

The owner knew that the only way to make his servant more valuable was to allow him to be stretched and let him discover his capacity for himself. This is the same process God uses in our lives to make us more valuable and to train us for our destinies.

> *Whoever can be trusted with very little can also be trusted with much, and whoever is dishonest with very little will also be dishonest with much.*
>
> —Luke 16:10

As I said in a previous chapter, there are no small assignments. You are going to grow through each one, and each one will add to your capacity for the next.

I have been through this process so many times. Each time, I am tempted to think, *No, I cannot do this. I do not know how,* or *I do not have time.* But each time I say, "Yes, I am stretched" and become more capable of reaching my potential.

People can look at my life and think, *Oh, it must be so easy to be out of debt, to be on television, to have a private plane. Wow, what a life.* Well, I will agree—what a life; it is a good life and a glorious life! But you do not know how my life got to where it is today. You do not know the perseverance it took, many times under extreme pressure, to rise to this level of capacity.

And I am still growing, and God keeps giving me even bigger assignments. I feel that I am constantly being stretched with bigger projects and stretched with needing more money to accomplish them. But I would not trade the pressure (and sometimes the chaos) for the world, for it is God's training system to help me accomplish all that I am called to accomplish.

If I could give you one piece of advice, it would be DON'T QUIT! Allow God to stretch you into the person you were meant to be.

God always comes through. He never fails. Your future is in front of you, and you must press on.

Will you allow God to stretch you?

I was at a Wednesday night prayer meeting. My daughter was leading prayer when she suddenly stopped, looked at me, and began to prophesy. This is what she said:

The Lord says, "The harvest is too big for you. I am stretching you. Only by My Spirit can you understand what is about to happen. Will you step out, let Me lead you to hard things beyond your understanding, the impossible?"

I thought, *Oh no, I know what this means.* It was not my first time out.

I appreciate the fact that God was asking me if I would allow Him to lead me into hard things, impossible things. I know they make for great stories when you have walked through them and that God always shows up.

But I also know the pain of stretching, the price to be paid to go somewhere you have never been before. But, and this is a big BUT, I also know of God's goodness and His promotion system, so I immediately said, "YES!"

God wants to bring the potential that He put in you out. That is the only way you will reach your destiny. He has to stretch you! How does God stretch us? *Pressure.*

If you blow up a balloon and then let the air out, the balloon is then stretched out; it is bigger. This is the same with you and me. Once we engage pressure and do not quit, our capacity grows. Capacity means bigger projects and bigger checks by the way. You know, it is fun talking about being generous until God tells you to give $100,000 away. Or give your favorite car away. Your trust in God has to grow, and your own capacity has to grow.

A few weeks after I said yes to God in that meeting, I found out what it was about. Our television broadcast, which was on a weekly, one day a week schedule, was offered a *daily* slot. That might sound great, but there are a few issues to navigate with that kind of change. First is that our airtime cost would go up 500% instantly, and we were just barely able to pay the weekly rate at that time. Second, we would have to produce and edit five programs a week, and we did not have a television department. At the time, we outsourced our one television program a week to a company that would come in and record four programs in a week for that current month. They would cut and edit the programs, ship the programs to the network, and do all the work. But then I realized I would need to move all that in house to manage it. And the bigger problem was that Drenda and I did not know how to build a TV department. But we scrambled to figure things out.

On the money side of the equation, we were still finishing the Now Center, our church campus, and there just was not any extra money to put into building television. On the production side, we had to buy camera equipment and hire the staff to run it. There were days that it looked impossible. But God was faithful and kept encouraging Drenda and me, and we pushed through.

Our biggest hurdle came about four months in when we found out we were half a million dollars behind on our airtime bills. That was especially hard because the name of our television program is *Fixing the Money Thing.*

I contemplated whether or not we would be able to stay on TV. I felt I could not continue with integrity if I could not pay the airtime bill. I had to battle many doubts at that time. But again, God is faithful, and Drenda was such an encouragement.

In a dream that week, God showed me that all of the bills would be paid in one lump sum, which I would have said would be impossible in the natural. But that weekend at church, all $500,000 came in, the airtime bills were caught up to current, and they have been current ever since.

Wow, it has been an incredible journey!!!!

We changed through that process. We now do *two* daily programs and spend millions to get the Gospel out. We look back at what we faced then, and it does not look as big as it did then. You always have to remember what we learned in chapter one: God's grace is working with you! Walking these years with God, I certainly understood why most of Paul's epistles start with the words:

"Grace and peace to you from God our Father and the Lord Jesus Christ."

We need to remember we are not alone. His grace, that supernatural empowerment, is working in our lives. It does take courage to say yes and to step into the unknown, but it is worth it; I can testify to that.

Drenda and I have traveled the world preaching the Gospel. We have seen every miracle recorded in the New Testament take place before our own eyes. We have seen thousands of people's lives changed and have eaten from the best of the land. There is no place better than purpose!

My prayer for you is that you abound in every good work that God gives you to do, and that you will remember how important being generous is.

In closing, here is one of my favorite psalms:

> *Praise the Lord. Blessed are those who fear the Lord, who find great delight in his commands. Their children will be mighty in the land; the generation of the upright will be blessed. Wealth and riches are in their houses, and their righteousness endures forever. Even in darkness light dawns for the upright, for those who are gracious and compassionate and righteous.*

Good will come to those who are generous and lend freely, who conduct their affairs with justice. Surely the righteous will never be shaken; they will be remembered forever. They will have no fear of bad news; their hearts are steadfast, trusting in the Lord. Their hearts are secure, they will have no fear; in the end they will look in triumph on their foes. They have freely scattered their gifts to the poor, their righteousness endures forever; their horn will be lifted high in honor. The wicked will see and be vexed, they will gnash their teeth and waste away; the longings of the wicked will come to nothing.

—Psalm 112:1-10

I love the part about the wicked being vexed. God always has the last word. Success is always the greatest vengeance.

If you know my story, you know that I basically flunked high school with a 1.3 grade point average. When God told me to go to college after He called me to preach, I was not looking forward to it.

In my first-year English class, I had to write a paper. My professor handed it back with a huge "F" on the front page and a note that said, "Is it possible that you even went to high school?" I had to have a tutor help me learn what I never learned in high school.

LEARN HOW THE KINGDOM OPERATES, AND YOU WILL ENJOY THE GOOD LIFE THAT GOD HAS PROMISED!

When my first book came out, I received an email from that English professor. It said, "Is it possible that this is the same Gary Keesee that I had in class?" He was so shocked to see that I had written a book.

Hey, let God and you shock all of your friends!

A person I went to high school with stopped by my financial

company's office one day and said, "I just don't get it. Gary flunked out of high school, and now he is on TV all over the world?"

I love stories like that, and God loves stories like that! So remember, your story is not finished. Strive to be generous as you represent God's heart wherever you go. Learn how the Kingdom operates, and you will enjoy the good life that God has promised!

—Gary Keesee

> *This service that you perform is not only supplying the needs of the Lord's people but is also overflowing in many expressions of thanks to God. Because of the service by which you have proved yourselves, others will praise God for the obedience that accompanies your confession of the gospel of Christ, and for your generosity in sharing with them and with everyone else. And in their prayers for you their hearts will go out to you, because of the surpassing grace God has given you. Thanks be to God for his indescribable gift!*

—2 Corinthians 9:12-15

If you would like to learn more about Forward Financial Group or our safe money investment strategies, visit forwardfinancialgroup.com or call us at 1-(800)-815-0818.

If would like to find out more about our Financial Revolution Conferences or if you would like to host a conference, please give us a call at (740) 964-7400 and ask for the executive office.